Introducing
Social Work

This book is due for return on or before the last date shown below.

Russell House

D1355023

First published in 2005 by:
Russell House Publishing Ltd.
4 St. George's House
Uplyme Road
Lyme Regis
Dorset DT7 3LS

Tel: 01297–443948
Fax: 01297–442722
e-mail: help@russellhouse.co.uk
www.russellhouse.co.uk

British Library Cataloguing-in-publication Data:

A catalogue record for this book is available from the British Library.

ISBN: 1–903855–52–7

Typeset by Saxon Graphics Ltd, Derby

Printed by Cromwell Press, Trowbridge

Russell House Publishing

Is a group of social work, probation, education and youth and community work practitioners and academics working in collaboration with a professional publishing team.

Our aim is to work closely with the field to produce innovative and valuable materials to help managers, trainers, practitioners and students.

We are keen to receive feedback on publications and new ideas for future projects.

Contents

Introduction

Steven M Shardlow and Peter Nelson

The decision to enter social work is a momentous one, as is any decision about which occupation to enter and where and how to build a career. This book is intended to assist: those considering a career in social work about whether to make that choice; those who are relatively new to social work and who want to find their bearings, orientate themselves within and to the profession; those at a early stage in their social work career and would like a concise overview of key areas of social work practice; those who are on placement in the United Kingdom, or living abroad and who need an introduction to social work in the UK.

Prospective students attending for interview, as part of the admission procedures for social work training, are commonly asked a question which seeks to test their knowledge and understanding of the profession they are hoping to join. The question may be couched in a variety of ways but is essentially asking the candidates for their views on: 'What is professional social work?' This book aims, amongst other things, to help candidates address that question, by providing both an introduction to key themes in social work, and reviewing policy and practice in central areas of social work, as they are practised in the various countries of the United Kingdom England, Northern Ireland, Scotland and Wales (not that we can assume social work will be identical in each of these countries).

In some ways, answering the question is straightforward; professional social work is what professional social workers do. What social workers do has in the past, and is likely again in the future, to vary depending on the particular historical, economic and political context. Furthermore, currently social workers may be employed in a variety of statutory or voluntary settings, they may work with adults or children, people with mental health problems or young offenders, but the nature of the task is reflected in their individual and collective practice. Yet just as prospective student social workers may struggle to convey the essence of the profession, so do many experienced practitioners when faced with the inevitable but uncomfortable question from friends, family or clients: 'What is it you actually do?'

One obstacle to answering the question is perhaps provided by the fact that there is arguably no discrete body of knowledge and skills that belongs only to social work. Social workers need to know about the law but so do lawyers. Social workers need to know about child development but so do health visitors, psychologists and many others. Social workers need to develop skills in interviewing and communication, they need to be able to use authority appropriately and wisely, but these skills are equally important for police officers.

There is apparently no particular body of knowledge and skills, which separates social workers from their colleagues in allied professions.

An alternative approach perhaps indicates a way forward towards answering the question. It is possible to think of social work as a constellation of knowledge and skills, where what is discrete to the social work profession is the coming together of clusters of specific knowledge and skills, some of which gain prominence at particular moments in time. For example, the knowledge of child development, parenting ability and the impact of environmental factors, alongside knowledge of the Children Act 1989 and agency and government policy, which are currently brought to bear in undertaking assessment work with children and their families. These clusters of knowledge and skills combine through social work theory and methods to define partially an individual's practice. The final defining factor, however, is perhaps the most important, in that this provides the centre of the constellation around which all the clusters of knowledge and skills orbit, that is social work values and a commitment to anti–oppressive practice.

Professional social work training has for many years required that workers are not only skilled and knowledgeable, but 'that they treat people with respect and are honest, trustworthy and reliable. They must be self aware and critically reflective, and their practice must be founded on, informed by and capable, of being judged against a clear value base' (CCETSW, 1998). In order to complete successfully a social work training course, candidates undertaking the Diploma in Social Work are required to demonstrate adherence and commitment to a number of value requirements. They must:

- Identify and question their own values and prejudices, and their implications for practice;
- Respect and value uniqueness and diversity, and recognise and build on strengths;
- Promote people's rights to choice, privacy, confidentiality and protection, while recognising and addressing the complexities of competing rights and demands;
- Assist people to increase control of and improve the quality of their lives, while recognising that control of behaviour will be required at times in order to protect children and adults from harm;
- Identify, analyse and take action to counter discrimination, racism, disadvantage, inequality and injustice, using strategies appropriate to role and context; and,
- Practise in a manner that does not stigmatise or disadvantage individuals, groups or communities.

(CCETSW, 1998: 7)

Within the new social work degree, the prescribed curriculum comprises three elements: the Requirements for Social Work Training, the National Occupational Standards for Social Work and the QAA Benchmark Statement for Social Work (DH,

2002: 2). A defining principle of the benchmark statement is that social work is a 'moral activity' and students must learn not only to 'understand the impact of injustice, social inequalities and oppressive social relations' but also to 'challenge constructively individual, institutional and structural discrimination' (QAA for Higher Education, 2000:12).

In the same way that social work knowledge and skills are shared with allied professions, arguably so is much of the profession's values. Similarly in the way that clusters of knowledge and skills gain prominence at particular historical conjunctures, so do the values at the centre of the profession. Yet in order to understand what social workers do, and perhaps equally importantly, how they practise, the key factor is that an adherence and commitment to social work values entails action. It is not sufficient to identify and analyse discrimination, racism, disadvantage, inequality and injustice. Social workers are required to 'take action to counter' that discrimination. It is perhaps this factor more than any other, which brings uniqueness to social work practice.

The definition of social work adopted by the International Federation of Social Workers in 2000 reflects the centrality of social work values:

The social work profession promotes social change, problem solving in human relationships and the empowerment and liberation of people to enhance well-being. Utilising theories of human behaviour and social systems, social work intervenes at the points where people interact with their environments. Principles of human rights and social justice are fundamental to social work.
(IFSW Montreal, Canada, July 2000)

The definition and the accompanying commentary use terminology and concepts, which firmly locate social work in the twenty-first century. The notion of human rights and social justice as the motivation and justification for social work activity indicates the continuity of a central value base driving social work throughout its history.

The IFSW argue that the holistic focus of social work is universal, but that the emphasis and priorities of social work practice will vary between countries and over time, dependant on historical, cultural and economic conditions. In collectively seeking to provide an introduction to professional social work the chapters in this book aim to identify and illustrate the specific clusters of knowledge, skills and values that have come together to define professional social work practice as it is currently practised in the United Kingdom.

However, the representations of social work in this book cannot provide a complete picture. Social work is such a diverse activity. Hence, in selecting the materials to include in this book there is much that has been left out as well as much that is included. To bring to life social work practice the book includes some chapters which reflect the freshness, immediacy and passion of practice and some that adopt an academic style – reviewing the available evidence for particular forms of practice. It is not just the content of the book that is grounded in the diversity of social work, so is the style of writing.

We hope you enjoy the book.

About the authors

Kathryn Mackay BA, MSc, CQSW qualified in 1984 and has worked in variety of settings including a psychiatric hospital and a community care team before joining the University of Stirling in 1997. She is an approved Mental Health Officer and an approved external assessor for MHO courses in Scotland. Her teaching and research interests are mental health, dementia and community care in general.

Peter Nelson is a Senior Lecturer in Social Work at Sheffield Hallam University; he has worked for many years as a social worker with children and families and as a specialist practice teacher. He has considerable experience of teaching and working in social work, much of this in direct contact with our target audience for the book.

Annette Rimmer is Associate Head (Teaching and Learning) in the School of Community, Health Sciences and Social Care at the University of Salford and a tutor at the University of Manchester (Community and Youth Work). Her background is in Community and Social Work. Her chapter is written together with service user colleagues in the CATS and YIPPEE groups. She has been actively involved in advocating for and writing about Citizen Participation since 1993 and continues to have close involvement with these two groups, who now have an international profile.

Cherry Rowlings is Professor of Social Work at the University of Stirling. Her research interests are community care, social work education in UK and continental Europe, social work with older people, residential work.

Steven M. Shardlow is Professor of Social Work at the University of Salford, England, where he is Director of Salford Centre for Social Work Research. In addition, he is Professor II in Social Work, at Bodø University College, Norway. He is the founding Editor-in-Chief of the *Journal of Social Work*. Previously, he has worked as a social work practitioner and manager. Current research interests are in the following areas: evidence-based policy and practice; professional ethics; comparative practice in the social professions; professional social work education and practice – especially in respect of practice learning. He has published widely in these fields, including eleven books; his work has been translated into several languages.

Cathy Spencer is a social worker who has worked in the field of learning disability for fifteen years. She is currently employed by the Association for Real Change, an organisation which supports providers of services for people with a learning disability. Cathy played a key role in the development of the Learning Disability Awards Framework (LDAF), a national strategy for improving the training of workers in learning disability services. Central to this she co-designed the nationally recognised Certificates in Working with People who have Learning Disabilities. Her current and future work on LDAF includes designing awards suitable for people with learning disabilities themselves, for informal carers, and for workers with children who have learning disabilities.

Kirsten Stalker BA, PhD, CQSW is a Reader at the Social Work Research Centre, University of Stirling. She was previously a Research Associate at the Norah Fry Research Centre, University of Bristol. Her research interests are in social models of disability, and ideas of choice, participation and inclusion. Much of her work has centred on eliciting the views of service users, particularly disabled people, people with learning disabilities and disabled children. She has published widely in the field of community care and disability.

Brian Williams is Professor of Community Justice and Victimology at De Montfort University, Leicester. His publications include *Working with Victims of Crime: Policies, Politics and Practice* (Jessica Kingsley, 1999).

Acknowledgements

We would like to thank colleagues within the social work team at Sheffield Hallam University (in particular Anne Hollows for her ideas and encouragement) and at the University of Salford for their continuing support and assistance. We are also grateful for the support of Liz Cresswell and the Graham Greene for secretarial assistance. Many people have contributed to this book, for example those who have assisted or inspired particular authors; there are too many to name, so we would like to thank them all.

Dedication

For Harry Nelson and Les Shardlow

Chapter 1

What is Professional Social Work? Social Work and Social Justice

Annette Rimmer[1]

Introduction

For those of us who have been working as social workers for many years, to answer the question, 'What is social work?' is both difficult and complex, as *social work* is so many different things practised in many places. Before discussing the nature of social work, there are two important messages to convey to newcomers. The first is a warm and genuine welcome to the work. The second is a warning, although a friendly warning, that social work is not 'just a job', it is much more *a way of life*. It is, however a way of life, which brings rich reward, as demonstrated by a service user's comments in *Community Care*, 'social workers saved my life' (Jerrom, 2001). One of the aims of this chapter is to present a 'clean sheet', which invites the reader to take part in a discussion about what social work has been, is now and should be in the future. Further, how, together with other important players, we can formulate a social work fit for the twenty-first century.

It is not the intention to negate the history of social work, but to use it as the foundation stone for our discussion. This chapter will examine aspects of social work history and also consider some recurring themes. One of these themes is the idea that some people deserve support and others do not, an idea that has bedevilled social welfare in the United Kingdom as:

> ...for Centuries, we divided the poor and unfortunate into two groups. The first were those who had fallen on calamities, which they could not help: the sick, the disabled, the widows, orphans ...that is broadly speaking, the deserving. The second group included offenders against the law, unmarried mothers, vagrants, the unemployed...broadly speaking, the undeserving.
>
> (Younghusband, 1964: 17)

There is no question that social work, in the present day, operates on the front line of 'social exclusion' and 'citizenship' – the current terminology used to refer to the issues surrounding who should receive help and who should not. Newcomers to

---

[1] This chapter was written in collaboration with Citizens as Trainers and YIPPEE

social work will want to debate and discuss their own definitions of these contentious concepts, which, at the time of writing have been defined by the 'new left' as being inextricably linked to *responsibilities and duties* in society in respect of employment, school attendance, law abidance, traditional family values and so on. In their attempt to describe what full citizenship and inclusion mean, the Labour Government have tiptoed (indeed sprinted) towards the 'old right'.

This chapter is grounded upon the principle that full citizenship and inclusion will only be achieved when excluded people have their say in the democratic process. For our purposes here, this entails defining what social work should be, as:

> *If social work is to be true to its stated professional ethic of self-determination and empowerment, then this must begin with the nature of its discussions about itself and service users. These must be participatory. Because of its potential impact upon them, any social policy research paradigm or agenda should be developed in close association with those included in the category of social exclusion.*
>
> (Beresford cited in Barry and Hallet, 1998: 96)

Hence, this chapter attempts to make paramount the voice of the service user as an essential point of the democratic process. People who use our services are hugely important in determining the nature of our new twenty-first century social work. Sadly, another recurrent theme has been that some citizens, particularly black citizens, have not been enabled to participate in the discourse which has defined and governed social work, due to the fact that, for example:

> *Black women's relationships with social workers have been fraught with antagonisms...we are constantly confronted with racist, classist or culturally biased judgements about our lives.*
>
> (Bryan et al., 1985: 112)

This chapter offers a variety of different perspectives about social work, as it exists today and diverse aspirations about what social work should be in the twenty-first century. It is offered as an invitation to discuss how new social workers might define, refine and develop their profession.

A Little History

Dame Eileen Younghusband is one of the most famous and prolific writers about the history of social work. As Martin Davies comments in his forward to one of her histories of social work, 'The Newest Profession' (1981: 1) her life as a social worker 'virtually spanned' the history of social work from 1870 to the 1980s. Social work, she writes: 'was born in the slums of London in the late-nineteenth Century' (1981: 3). She also made the hugely important connection that the history of social work is inextricably linked with the history of poverty and the history of women.

Still today, it is overwhelmingly women who are on the frontline of social work practice, both as service users and as workers (Dominelli and McLeod, 1989; Hanmer and Statham, 1991; Brook and Davis, 1985).

The birth of our profession occurred against a backdrop of poverty and disease, in a dramatically unequal society where women and children had few rights. It was a period marked by colonialism, especially of the 'Majority World' (Africa and Asia); a period when the enslavement of black people was only recently questioned.

When we look at the early 'Domestic Angels', the 'middle class lady almoners', like the Pankhursts, who initiated welfare work, we could easily criticise them for appearing as missionaries at home and abroad. They would present alms with one hand and a Christian Bible in the other. However, had it not been for their social conscience and subsequent social action, community and social work as we know it today, would not exist.

From the early beginnings of social work, distinct issues arose, which are still discussed on social, community and youth work courses. The first has already been mentioned; that the almoners decided who was deserving of help and who was not. Those who drank or stole would not be offered help and even the deserving were monitored closely, lest they turn into scroungers and become dependent upon alms. The Charity Organisation Society (COS), set up in 1869, was designed to organise social services and to keep records (now called case files) in order that aid was not duplicated. In case notes today, one can still find evidence of 'rationing' help and judgemental statements about people who appear to be 'manipulating' the system:

Tracey is a manipulative and promiscuous fifteen-year-old. She is constantly asking for money for new clothes and nights out. Furthermore, her mother wears too much cheap jewellery.

(Example from my own practice)

The social work role adopted by these 'ladies' was also to teach middle class mothering skills, budgeting skills and Christian worship to the 'women', many of whom were now working in factories, mills and mines spawned by the Industrial Revolution.

It is a moot point whether social work still retains these seemingly arrogant and oppressive attitudes. In his report on services for black mental health service users in Southampton, Angus Igwe (1998: 35) conveys the views of a professional, 'We must learn to step down (in a safe way) from the 'God's throne' and talk with (not at) those that matter'. It is also debatable that services for those judged as 'deserving' are better resourced than those for the 'undeserving'. Those of us who have worked for substance misuse agencies or in services for offenders and ex-offenders (groups vulnerable of being perceived as undeserving) have noted just how difficult it is to secure charity or government funding.

Questions may be asked about how much social work, as a professional activity, is taken seriously by society. We began as ad-hoc groups of 'do-gooding ladies,' but even though it is over 100 years since we organised ourselves, we have never gained the same respect or financial recognition, as have many other public servants. At the time of writing, the Government has launched a £2m campaign to attract people to our profession. However, according to Jerrom, 'This boost to social work recruitment is dwarfed by the sums spent to promote police, health service and education recruitment' (Jerrom, 2001). It could be that the overwhelmingly female character of social work (indicated by the ratio of female to male social workers) has had an impact upon the measure of respect we have achieved. Certainly, social work, particularly residential work has been, and still is, often seen as 'the natural work of women'.

Nevertheless, there were distinct philosophies of social work in the late nineteenth century, and though more subtle in their manifestation, those competing philosophies remain present today. Put very simply; there were social workers who worked for the COS, visiting huge families in overcrowded slum dwellings, offering cooking skills and bible readings. In 1872, Mary Carpenter defined social workers thus: 'They are single women who will be able to bestow their maternal love on those who are made to be pitied' Younghusband (1981: 19). Mary Richmond later defined social workers as 'Social Doctors' who diagnosed the causes of social failure and prescribed treatments (Richmond, 1917). This 'medical model' of social work is certainly still with us, not just in the fields of Disability and Mental Health, as discussed in later Chapters five and six, but also as a dominant, over-reaching philosophy.

> *Why do social workers treat me like a 'medical condition' just because I am disabled? Social work is about working together in partnership with everyone concerned. It's about getting away from the medical model, but instead taking on an holistic view of a client's situation.*
>
> (C, from Citizens as Trainers, 2001)

A different view of social work is present in the Christian Socialist and Suffragette movement; members of these groups believed that the social worker's role was to tackle root causes and improve living conditions for those in poverty. They campaigned for better housing, better pay and working conditions and most important of all, for the enfranchisement of *all* men and women. These social workers were community activists and campaigners. A visit to the Pump House museum in Manchester reveals something of what this means in practice as exemplified through the life of Hannah Mitchell in 1890. As a poor woman living in Tameside, she writes:

> *On one evening per week, the almoner visits me and looks after my children, so that I can attend a Suffragette meeting.*

Hannah provides a good example of the important role of social workers have in politicising service users. (Of course, it works both ways, as service users liberate and politicise us!) Hannah began as a woman living in poverty and eventually became a Poor Law Guardian and campaigner for women's rights. A further example is introduced by Emmeline Pankhurst, who was a Poor Law Guardian of the Manchester workhouse. She began her office by making sweeping changes, which meant better food and clothing for poor children, and older people who wore flimsy summer clothes throughout the year. 'The fact that bronchitis was epidemic among them, had not suggested to the male guardians any change of fashion of their clothes' (Mackenzie, 1975: 10). Within five years, she had 'changed the face of the earth for them, establishing a school, gymnasium and swimming bath' (ibid.). Later, she became frustrated with these 'perfunctory' changes and decided that this work was inadequate. 'We shall have to have *new laws* and it soon became apparent to me that we can never hope to get them until women have the vote'. Women guardians had striven in vain to have the Poor Law reformed 'in order to ameliorate conditions which break the hearts of women to see, but which apparently affect men very little' (ibid.). During the First World War, Emmeline's daughter Sylvia, the revolutionary socialist of the family, made passionate appeals on behalf of those who were left at home without breadwinners. 'She set up and worked in mother and baby clinics, fought for separation allowances, old age pensions, rights for unmarried mothers, war babies, sweated workers, equal pay for women in factories, victimised aliens and pacifists' (Mackenzie, 1975: 11). She epitomised the dual role of social workers as practical helpers and political activists.

So the debate continues today! Are we here to offer individual help to change and strengthen people or are we here to raise people's political consciousness, to enable them to fight for their rights and make society more equal? On the other hand, should we be doing both? As Clark admits:

> *...it would be ludicrous to suggest that social workers could achieve this all on their own, with the meagre resources at their disposal. However, they are in daily contact with the only untapped force in the social-democratic system – the citizen.*
>
> (Clark, 2000: 1)

Do we waste too often this unique position, an opportunity, with reasons, which amount to defeatism? Certainly, Thompson is clear where social work should aim:

> *Social work should support people in their struggles to break free from the disadvantage, discrimination and oppression they experience as a result of their social location.*
>
> (Thompson, 2000: 23)

Emmeline Pankhurst's comments about how women and men perceive social problems still resonate today. Amongst many social workers, there is a strongly held feminist belief that improving women's status and enabling them to be independent rather than dependent will improve life for men, women and children. It is still lamentably true that much social policy and, 'social work practice defines women as wives, mothers, carers, adolescent girls...and not as people' (Hanmer and Statham, 1988: 1). In 1924, Eleanor Rathbone, who fought for women to have a Child Allowance, wrote about women being especially disadvantaged:

> *Nothing can justify the subordination of one group of producers, the mothers –*
> *to the rest, and their deprivation of all share in the wealth of a community,*
> *which depends on them for its very existence.*
>
> (Cited in Pahl, 1989: 154)

Returning to our history of social work, and moving forward to the 1950s, we were convinced by Harold Macmillan, Prime Minister, that we had 'never had it so good'. After the formation of the Welfare State, we had conquered the 'five giants' of poverty, disease, ignorance, squalor and idleness. This allowed social workers to dispose of the almoner and missionary role, in favour of becoming therapists. There is a parallel with our counterparts in North America, who from the 1930s became enchanted by the theories of Freud:

> *In Britain, the post war welfare state arising from earlier parliamentary and*
> *labour struggles, was thought to assure most people of adequate income*
> *security, so that any problems of poverty remaining, would be largely*
> *behavioural and require one to one counselling.*
>
> (Liffman, 1978: 78)

Casualties of society could undergo social work 'treatment', which would change and strengthen their personalities. Social workers in the United Kingdom took on the ideas of psychotherapy, psychoanalysis and social learning.

The influence of Freud upon social work practice, cannot be underestimated, but even those who promote his ideas today, warn against Freudism, Eriksonism, Kleinism, Bowlbyism etc. as singular, unquestioned approaches upon which to ground professional practice:

> *As late as 1993, it is argued that 'many social work students were still being*
> *taught a narrow syllabus based on Freud's original schema...*
>
> (Brearley cited in Lishman, 1993: 55)

This approach enabled the service user to reflect upon their childhood and life experiences and through understanding begin to improve themselves and their circumstances. These psychodynamic approaches have enriched the landscape of social work practice and been adapted to include reflection on power and oppression. However, the idea that the generic social worker had the skills (or indeed the time) required to act as an analyst or therapist, began to lose popularity during the late 1960s in the United Kingdom.

During the 1960s, social work rediscovered poverty and social workers, who were using solely psychodynamic approaches, came under fire. How could an individual 'talking session' session stop the water coming in through the roof? (Benn, 1973: 36). Many social workers thought that this kind of social work was soul destroying:

Casework, in the context of poverty starts with an insurmountable disadvantage. There is growing evidence that service without a basic level of income wastes the efforts of the helpers.

(ibid.)

Here Benn echoes the frustrations of Christian socialists and the Pankhursts.

As part of a radical outburst Bailey and Brake amongst others condemned the psychodynamic way of doing social work, which they said 'helps clients come to terms as individuals with basically unacceptable situations' (1975: 145). Bryan et al. (1985) echoed this account by describing social workers as 'parasites' who perpetuated the very problems they were sent to alleviate. Having worked in the 'Freudian era', sometimes spending years working with the same person or family, I have to ask myself, did we too often overlook the root causes of people's low self esteem and depression? Should we have looked more closely at the impact of poverty, racism, sexism, homophobia, and ageism; and should we have done more to challenge the systems, which perpetuate disempowerment?

In the 1960s and 1970s, social work became much more concerned with structural problems and community activism, whereby social workers should enable service users to 'change their situation by collective action. We can only do this by acting collectively ourselves' (Bailey and Brake, 1975). It was during this era, that the Seebohm report (Report of the Committee on Local Authority and Allied Personal Social Services [Seebohm Report] 1968) was published. The report led to the amalgamation of different 'specialist' departments. Social workers became generalists, working with the full range of service users – rather than specialists[2]. Social workers worked in neighbourhoods, working with people and families holistically. The unity of social work was further confirmed in 1971 through the establishment of the Central Council for Education and Training (CCETSW), the body responsible for the regulation of social work training. Subsequently, the Barclay Report (Barclay, 1982) defined social workers as community developers whose functions included gaining resources and initiating community groups.

---

[2] In 1970, mental health workers, child care, medical and welfare workers joined together under the umbrella of the British Association of Social Workers.

Moving into the Twenty-First Century

To simplify our understanding of the nature and development of social work, Payne identifies three distinct categories of social work, which provide a useful reference point. We have, he says, a choice of: social work which is *individualist and reformist*, in other words 'it is an activity geared towards meeting social welfare needs on an individualized basis'; social work which is *socialist-collectivist*, meaning that it is:

> ...*part of a system which seeks to promote co-operation in society so that the most oppressed and disadvantaged people can gain power over their own lives; and finally, work that is reflexive-therapeutic; an approach 'geared towards promoting and facilitating personal growth in order to enable people to deal with the suffering and disadvantage they experience.*
>
> (Payne cited in Thompson, 2000: 12)

Some of us might prefer to select a single definition from these options as a description of ourselves; others would say that we try to combine all three options as social workers. Contrary to popular belief, this combination does not require super-human social workers, but workers committed to the application of a variety of interpersonal skills and the development of political awareness. Nevertheless, there are still those who think social work is too comfortably and complacently placed in the sphere of maintaining the equilibrium of individuals' relationship to wider society. McLeod and Bywaters (2000: 5) believe that this 'maintenance' model of social work implicates us in the maintenance of inequalities. While the Centre for Social Action states that we still overlook societal causes of individual misery. Members call for social workers to take on the principles of social action:

> *Social action is about users taking action for empowerment. Our practise should reflect the fact that oppression, social policy and the environment are much stronger factors in service user's lives than personal factors.*
>
> (Social Action Journal, 1995: 2)

A good example of socialisation can be found in Bandana Ahmad's book 'Black Perspectives in Social Work' (1993), where a black child is truanting from school. Ahmad suggests (1993: 51) that as social workers, our task is not simply to persuade the child back to school, but to examine underlying causes of their truancy. If, for example, racist bullying is the reason behind truancy, we need to challenge that with the school, not simply work with the child and force conformity. Otherwise, are we not simply blaming the victim? Nevertheless, social workers need a dual approach, they need theories and methods that work towards improving self-esteem and confidence, and theories and methods, which tackle societal root causes of problems. The social worker who becomes a 'political robot' spouting socialist rhetoric which ignores the individual's need for affection, genuine care and dignity, is as frightening as the one who becomes an a-political, kindly, but non-committal listener.

During the 1980s in the UK, there was a rise in unemployment, an increase in the numbers of lone parents and older people, many cuts were made in housing, social security and maternity benefits. State social work was forced to enter the market economy with financial charges made to individuals for help, support and housing. Many social workers in Mental Health and Older people's services became 'care managers' who bought packages of care for people, instead of providing that care themselves. The 1990 NHS Community Care Act was arguably a Government led return to individual casework. Services were organised around a distinction between those purchasing and those providing services. In addition, the Government could be seen as attempting to 'de-professionalise' the work by encouraging the employment of cheaper, unqualified 'care managers' to take over the social work role. This issue is debated and an alternative view proposed by Mackay in Chapter six of this book.

The social costs of the Conservative Government's welfare policies have been borne disproportionately by the poor, particularly women and black people (Williams, 1989: 168). Other oppressed groups were also aggrieved. 'Clause 28', (an amendment to the 1971 Local Government Act) prevented teachers, social and youth workers from informing children and young people about diversity in sexuality. Older people found that their pensions were no longer earnings related. Travellers and asylum seekers could be arrested under new justice policies. Disabled people felt their rights were eroded further. The new 'poll tax' upset so many people that it culminated in a huge collective backlash from citizens.

As a result of these oppressive policies, collective movements gained strength, unity and campaigned strongly for their rights. Disabled, gay, black and older people actively fought to be involved in policy making. The words of Paulo Freire (1972) became relevant as oppressed people joined together in order to liberate themselves and their oppressors. In social work, we had to listen to these groups and once again, change the way we worked. During and after the 1980s new social work, sociology and social policy books were published about black perspectives (Ahmad, 1990; Dominelli, 1989; 1990; Gilroy, 1987; Sivanandan, 1987); about Feminist perspectives (Brook and Davis, 1988; Hanmer and Statham,1985; Dominelli and McLeod, 1989; Glendinning and Millar, 1987) about Disability and Mental Health perspectives (Morris, 1996; Oliver, 1990; Pilgrim and Rogers, 1993); about general 'Anti-Oppressive' practice and service-user-participation and 'Empowerment' (Thompson, 1997; Dalrymple and Burke, 1995; Beresford and Croft, 1993; Langan and Lee, 1989).

Hence, in the 1980s and 1990s both social policy and citizenship movements influenced the social work role greatly. Whilst on the one hand, much state social work has become more market economy orientated, individualised and strictly targeted; on the other hand the government and many charity and campaigning organisations are funding more collective community action projects. This means that qualified social and community workers alike have a much wider range of exiting posts for which they might apply. For example, Dr. Barnardo's orphanages have disappeared and Barnardo's today provide a range of community action projects which seek to tackle neighbourhood poverty with credit unions, food co-ops and support groups. These projects aim to empower service users to gain the knowledge and confidence to help themselves and each other, rather than 'treat' users, with 'the traditional medical models' of social work which employ a pseudo-medical approach. See for example the discussion in respect of disability in Chapter five and of mental health in Chapter six.

The 1990s can be characterised as the decade of service user or citizen-participation, partnership and empowerment. Mayo cites the Human Development Report (1993) a global account of our situation as human beings compiled by The United Nations.

The best route is to unleash people's entrepreneurial spirit – to take risks, to compete, to innovate, to determine the direction and pace of development... people's participation is becoming the central issue of our time.

(Mayo, 1995: 2)

Section 46 of the NHS Community Care Act (90) demands that services should be organised in consultation with service users. This section and the 'uprising' of service users have led to the creation of citizen participation or service user involvement posts in some local authorities. It has become:

...increasingly difficult for government and service providers to ignore these local, regional and national organisations of people with sensory impairments, people with learning disabilities, survivors of the mental health system, people affected by HIV and older people. They (already) provide service users with their own distinct collective voices as well as support, self-help and opportunities to speak for themselves.

(Beresford and Harding, 1993: 11)

For over twenty years, writers such as Beresford, Morris, Harding and Croft, have challenged social workers to change the dominant culture of their profession. They formulated practical ways through which we could achieve genuine service user or citizen participation, not just in their own personal or family 'care' plans, but also through the creation and control of new effective services. Such writers point out the barriers to what was perceived as a 'revolutionary' approach and it quickly emerges that the most impenetrable barrier was our resistance as workers, teachers and managers. As Freire, Gramsci, Marx and others told us: *those with power, do not give it away easily, it is up to us to support service users in order that they can take power.*

*It isn't the bloody revolution which promises to change everything and leave us
(as service users) excluded just the same. It isn't the prescriptive policy that's
meant to improve our lot, but stigmatises and makes us dependent...the
smallest steps will take us forward, so long as we keep heading in the right
direction.*

(Beresford and Croft, 1993: 42)

Service users and workers who have been involved in this 'revolution' have
become experts in dealing with the barriers, which are located in themselves, in
social work training, in social work management and in government. This
movement is now strong and experienced, and a growing research literature is
evolving, which cannot and indeed should not be ignored.

The challenge is for social workers to be *partners* with service users, when so
many workers remain steeped in the 'treatment model' of social work and when
many of us feel too exhausted by our individual casework to do anything more
political or creative. This objective is difficult to achieve, as Doel and Shardlow
comment.

*The power relationship is not one that ends at the level of service user and
social worker. Workers themselves can feel a lack of power in relation to their
organisations, where decision-making and policy making can feel remote.
Students of social work...need to consider the question of empowerment – the
barriers and the opportunities – in relation to workers in the agency as well as
the users of the services.*

(Doel and Shardlow, 1998: 185)

Service Users' Viewpoints

It is time now to hear those citizens who use our services. The new social work of
the twenty-first century should be defined by people who use social work services?
K who has spent much of her life in the care system, laughed a little at this idea:

*TOPSS[3] (Training Organisations for the Personal Social Services) asked us to give
our opinions about what skills new social workers should have. They sent us
half a tree through the post – a big batch of papers. That put me off, but even
worse, there was no blank page – they had already decided what social
workers should be. It was all jargon and I spent hours trying to understand it.
It's typical, social workers think they already know what we want, so why
bother asking us?*

(K, member of YIPPEE[4] Group, 2001)

---

[3] Details of TOPSS (England) can be found at the following web address www.topss.org.uk
[4] Details of YIPPEE can be found at the following web addresses: www.yippee-group.org.uk
www.careleaders.org

Despite the 'explosion of enthusiasm' for citizen participation, highlighted by Beresford and Croft (1993), we have sadly, managed to exclude citizens from effective involvement in the provision of social work, by various means over the years. Using social work, medical and political jargon has been just one method of exclusion and as K points out later that 'these are nice people and they really want us to take part, but they are so used to speaking and writing with these long words, that they don't know they're doing it'.

Citizens who use social services are the most important stakeholders and in this chapter, I was determined to give them a voice. However, when asking citizens what they think social work is and what it should be, we should not be afraid of learning some 'home truths'. As P said:

> We have some great ideas about social work and I currently have a fantastic down-to-earth social worker, but I want you to know that I've had some terrible times with social workers. Please don't ask me to 'dress up' my experiences. When you ask us this question, expect to listen to the negatives too?
>
> (P, member of CATS Group, 2001)

Lindow emphasises the visionary nature of service users: 'Giving a vision for the future is a tall order...but as a psychiatric survivor perhaps I have more chance. We are good at visions' (Lindow, 1993: 23).

In my twenty-year search for best practice in social work, my most influential teachers have been service users. Without being patronising, they have also been my main source of support and humour in what is sometimes a frightening and dangerous job...frightening because of our immense power; dangerous because if we misuse that power, we could destroy lives. This section is designed, not to attack social work, but to convey a sense of reality. We should lament that we have so far failed to achieve the ideal (some would say idealistic) notion that service users are truly our partners, or our advisors. In this chapter it is argued that, perhaps controversially that they should be our managers...and *not* the other way round.

R brings out the importance of the need to develop true partnership:

> Before I ever saw or met a social worker, I wondered what their role was. I had a picture in my head: nice car, talks posh, dresses very smartly, usually wearing black with a brief case. I got my social worker and felt completely overpowered, I never got a say. Even though I was asked, I panicked and couldn't think from the top of my head what I wanted. I felt too young to talk. I never felt I had no power. Knowing someone else, who wasn't my mother, was going to take over my life – a stranger. What is your role? You tell me. How could you support me? What about the future? Where will I be in ten years? Are you going to try and change me? Am I no good as I am?
>
> (R, member of YIPPEE Group, 2001)

R expresses the shock she felt that someone who was coming to help suddenly took control of her life and did not ensure that her voice was heard. Is anyone 'too young' to have a voice and is it not our job to make sure they *do* have one?

Similarly, the worker who entered A's life brought bewilderment: '*When I first saw a social worker, I actually thought it was my dad's new girlfriend*' (A, a member of YIPPEE group, 2001). Clearly, we need to be able to explain to people exactly what our role is. How can we do this if we are not sure of our role for ourselves? Another element conveyed so well by A, is the intimacy of the social work role. We often see people in their own homes, 'sit on their settees' and expect them to talk about extremely personal and private issues. Though the law sometimes gives us a right to do this, we should constantly ask ourselves if this is really any of our business. Have I made a good enough relationship with this person to ask such things? Would I want a stranger to know all this about me?

Daljit, a service user with learning disabilities gives an important message for new social workers:

> *I want you to think how it feels when you're sat across the table from me, while my life has been laid out for you to pick at. My home, my lifestyle, my failed relationships, my mistakes, the times I've been so exhausted and threatened I've wanted to give up – its all there. Your life, on the other hand, is kept private, hidden, protected. You don't have to feel this exposed, this vulnerable. I'm imperfect but I'm trying to do the right thing. If we just talked about what most of us want from our lives – somewhere permanent and decent to live, to love and be loved, to feel worthwhile. Our hopes and dreams are as important and real as anyone else's.*
>
> (Daljit, a service user with learning disabilities, CATS, 2001)

C a disabled woman, reminds us of elements of social work history and challenges the idea that social workers are here to diagnose and treat social ills:

> *Why do people like us become a tick in a box, a number on a computer, a statistic? Why am I suddenly a medical condition? When did I stop being a person? I can assure everyone I am just as human, with thoughts and feelings like everyone else. Social work should be about getting away from the medical model and instead taking on a holistic view of us as people. We have hopes and wishes just like you. It's not us and them. Social workers should be our partners.*
>
> (C, a service user, 2001)

This comment also illustrates the perceived division of the social world between *us and them*. Citizens who use services have skills, talents, political ideals, dreams and aspirations. Our role should be to help them realise and achieve those things, not to consider ourselves as superior. Mullender and Ward stress that although social workers may employ special skills and knowledge, 'these do not accord privilege and are not solely the province of workers' (1995: 16). Today, many more social workers are people who have used services and because of their life experiences, they bring a wealth of skills, knowledge, understanding and compassion to the profession. Part of our role must be to build their confidence and ensure that they have opportunities to achieve their ambitions.

> *I was brought up in care. My main memory as a teenager, is of constantly being accused of lying – of being wantonly or otherwise disbelieved. The experience was one of disempowerment to maintain what the social workers considered should be the status quo. Social work then and now is neither about individual nor social improvement. Social work should be about empowerment of people to improve their lot, end their personal suffering and fulfil their goals.*
>
> (Phil Frampton, Care Leavers Association, 2001)

These comments resonate with those of Frampton who highlights the 'maintenance' role of social work; the idea that we 'help individuals' with their personal problems to adjust as well as possible to the society around them' (Payne cited *in* Dominelli et al., 1998). Another member of YIPPEE comments as follows:

> *I became a client of social services when I was two years old, due to neglect and cruelty. I am forty-six now and have used all the services you can imagine, including having over eighty treatments of ECT (electro convulsive therapy). I've had some bad workers, but now I have an excellent one. She's articulate, she consults with me about everything properly and doesn't do what she thinks best, she listens to me and cares. She respects me even though I have done wrong in the past. Because of her respect and encouragement I have now become a trainer and consultant for social services. Without respect, I think I would have committed suicide, now I'm helping to change services so they listen more.*
>
> (J, member of YIPPEE, 2001)

J clearly demonstrates the importance of social workers working to promote and enable full participation in systems. Just as Hannah Mitchell's almoner encouraged her to join the suffragettes and become a poor law Guardian; J has found a worker who treats her as an equal. They raise each other's political consciousness and J realises her huge potential. The gains are both personal and political. Beresford and Turner speak about the enormous, yet devalued contribution made by service users to the welfare state. Not only as paid workers and volunteers, but also financially:

> *Please stress in all you publish and distribute that we all have a giving role at some stage in our lives and nobody is only a 'giver' or only a 'receiver'.*
>
> (Older woman quoted in Beresford and Turner, 1997: 52)

Social workers have another extremely important and dramatic role in people's lives; we are often involved in *moving people* from one home to another, from their current life to a different life:

> *I never saw much of my second social worker, but I did understand a bit more about social workers. He wasn't around much and left us in places (foster care and residential homes) without saying how long we was going to be there for and without phoning.*
>
> (A, member of YIPPEE, 2001)

A not only brings out, once again, the intimacy of our involvement, but the part we play in crucial and often traumatic moves; from home to foster care, to psychiatric hospital, to hospices, to residential or sheltered housing. In terms of theories and methods that inform our work, understanding grief, loss and life changes are central to that work. Only then can we fulfil our role, to ensure that service users are full participants in any life changing decisions or plans. Everything should be explained and prepared for in a way that is understood. Young children need to be involved by social workers in decision-making, yet we often underestimate their ability to understand, as William (aged six) protests:

> *It's not fair! The big people are doing what they like, but they won't let us do what we like. They think that because we're small, we don't have brains. But we do – we've got big brains! What I think is people's brains get smaller when they grow up.*
>
> (Miller, 1997: 5)

The YIPPEE group (care-leaver-trainers) have an exercise, which they devised for use in the training of new and qualified social workers. In the exercise, they ask: *How many addresses have you had in your life? Go on, work it out.* After feedback (which generally elicits that people have five or six) they give information about their own lives in comparison:

> *We are aged between seventeen and twenty-one and some of us have had over sixty different addresses! When you are put in a foster home, you often aren't allowed to have moods or argue like 'normal children', because they'll ring the social worker and ask them to take you away.*
>
> (YIPPEE group, 2001)

The group give us the sense that most of us actually have little idea how it feels to be moved around so much, losing our few possessions, our school, our beloved friends and feeling blamed and punished. We can learn much from service users about these feelings:

> *Social workers should be good listeners. They should always put things in non-jargon language. They should always involve us, our friends, family and pets in*

any assessment they make of us. You might laugh, but pets are very important companions for so many of us older people.

(S, member of CATS, 2001)

S establishes important details which we need to hear and not trivialise. It is not for us as social workers to prioritise which issues are important in people's lives:

Just because you as a social worker want your life to be a certain way, that doesn't mean we are the same as you. But, in some ways we are the same because though we may be older or disabled, we still want a good job, a good social life, love, sex, lots of friends…these things are not the preserve of social workers, so its really important to think 'would I want that for me, for my children, for my partner, for my friend? If the answer to these questions is 'NO', you can bet your bottom dollar that the service user doesn't want it either.

(S, member of CATS, 2001)

It is evident then, that from examining *what social work is not*, we learn a great deal about what it is. All of the people who contributed here had extremely positive advice about what social work should be. This advice, from young and older people, from black and white people who have used a myriad of services, centres upon the ideal of a social worker who is not too arrogant to *listen and learn from them.*

Women and particularly black women have been at the forefront of community action and social care (Naples, 1998; Dominelli, 1990). 'White social workers don't always understand what it's like to be mixed race and in care, but if they listen, they can learn from us' (N, member of YIPPEE, 2001). Of course, this is not a substitute for actively training and recruiting more black professionals, but N's point suggests that white workers should not feel awkward or afraid of working with black people, provided that they are prepared to learn. Racism in social work is sometimes manifested when social workers fail to offer any service at all to black citizens, through fear of getting it wrong.

A constant theme in our discussion was the idea that social workers need to have a sense of fun:

My ideal social worker would have to be someone that I could rely on, someone who could explain things to me, someone who is non-judgemental (long word for me), someone to have a laugh with and is friendly.

(A, member of YIPPEE, 2001)

When people seek support, they have often coped for many years without our help and one of the most effective coping strategies involves humour. We should not allow ourselves to be completely problem orientated, but should seek relationships with people which bring out their (and our) strengths, skills, talents and humour.

People will not respect us more if we present ourselves as perfect, serious professionals. We need to show our human, sometimes vulnerable and fun-loving selves.

Another requirement for good social work is flexibility, as Hillman and Mackenzie comment:

> *As a social worker, you will need to feel secure enough to be flexible. You will need to cultivate a resilience and humour that allow you to take setbacks in your stride. The improvements we all hope to see in both clients and services come slowly and sometimes not at all.*
>
> (Hillman and Mackenzie, 1993: 18)

On this note, AH gave the following serious, yet humorous view of social workers:

> *They are:*
> *Useful and harmless,*
> *Useful and harmful*
> *Useless and harmless or*
> *Useless and harmful*

AH goes on to say:

> *I believe the most useful functions of good social workers these days are in the areas of bringing to non-medical factors some weight and credence when people are having their needs assessed …additionally, I think the role of social worker as broker of services is potentially very fruitful and can lead to a fuller inclusion of people in ordinary community activities and citizenship.*
>
> (AH, Distress Awareness Training Agency, 2001)

One potentially daunting feature of social work is the amount of knowledge with which social workers are expected to be familiar, as Hillman and Mackenzie note:

> *The knowledge base that is potentially relevant (in social work) is endless…the key to coping with this lies not in knowing it all, but in knowing enough to know whom to ask and where to look.*
>
> (Hillman and Mackenzie, 1993: 42)

It is important that we see ourselves as gatherers of national and local resources. AH's comment above that social workers are 'brokers' of services refers to the fact that we can be very useful in directing people to a group or organisation, which may be more helpful than direct intervention by ourselves. Our role may be for example in supporting someone to attend a Mental Health Forum, Disability Rights or Care Leavers' group. As a recent social work student comments, 'Social Workers are signposts' (Mick Gayle, social work student 2001). Sometimes a signpost is enough, at other times we need to build confidence by going a little way on the journey to support people. After all, as Paulo Freire found, when people are powerless for a length of time, they internalise all those insidious ideas of worthlessness, and helplessness (Freire, 1972).

We are not a piece of paper, a file or a case number. Anyone who works with people, should let them know that they are somebody and they are special.

(K, member of YIPPEE, 2001)

At the time of writing, there is a national shortage of qualified workers, which has taken its toll on the standard of the service and on the stress levels of overworked colleagues. Social workers need to care for themselves both personally and politically. In other words, we need to balance our work with pleasure and relaxation. Furthermore, we need to ensure that we are neither undervalued nor exploited. We can do this by seeking support from like-minded colleagues, service users and becoming active trade unionists. We need to work collectively to protect ourselves and to lobby for more resources from government and management. If we are working to empower citizens, we must first empower ourselves. Black workers, women workers, disabled workers, gay workers are not immune from the pressures of living in an oppressive society. Brooks and Davis (1985), Hanmer and Statham (1988), Dominelli and McLeod (1989) have written particularly about women's need to steel themselves against the white patriarchal management of social services:

I've learned a lot on the social work course. I've learned how to support other students and how they support me. I've learned to challenge effectively without being aggressive, how to communicate using 10,000 words when one would have done. Most importantly how to step back from situations. I have a much wider perspective and have learned that children in residential homes are not a homogeneous group, but are individuals, not case studies, but individuals. I already knew this, but managers tried to tell me otherwise.

(Y social work student, Salford University, 2001)

As Y comments above 'challenging' does not require aggression, but the positive use of assertiveness. The importance of this is emphasised by P:

Social workers should fight for what we want. Sometimes their managers say 'No' because they haven't got the money, but social workers need to challenge them on our behalf. I have a good social worker who I trust will take the time to fight for me. She is strong and assertive. She understands what I want.

(P, member of CATS, 2001)

Of course, there are many conflicts and stresses within the social work role. We are often the piggy-in-the-middle between service user and manager; or as Dominelli writes 'negotiators between communities and the state' (1990). Social policy and budget designation may force service users to compete with each other for vital services. Competing for resources dilutes the strength of service users, the organisations they lead and their social workers (Chorcora et al., cited in Dalrymple and Burke, 1995: 31).

Social workers have a role in challenging such policies with the support of service users, via their managers, and by linking service users to wider campaign groups in society. P is a good example of someone who now belongs to a variety of political and pressure groups; similar to many other citizens writing here, she 'suffered' some ineffective social workers, then met one who put her in touch with support and campaign groups:

This is the reason you are reading my words now. Prior to this, I never left the house because I am a wheelchair user, am registered blind and have mental health problems. Social workers in the past thought I was helpless and would not want to leave the house. Then, a social worker empowered me to join Survivors groups and a few years ago, the CATS group (Citizens as Trainers). I am now the chair of CATS and SIS (Survivors in Salford). Social workers should get money to start groups. We will support you to do this and we will run the groups ourselves. We just need you to kick-start the process.

(P, member of CATS, 2001)

Dave Ward, an academic and member of the Centre for Social Action was shocked when in 1998 he was invited to write about social workers as initiators of groups. 'Where has groupwork gone?' (Cited in Adams et al., 1998: 149). Of course, some social workers have always been involved in groupwork, but his reaction reminds us how powerful has been the doctrine of individualised social work since the 1980s. As an opposing tension, groupwork can be seen as essentially democratic and empowering: 'it has a place at the centre of democracy if involvement, participation and empowerment are to be totems rather than tokens' in social work (Ward, cited in Kemshall and Littlechild, 2000: 33). The citizens, who have contributed to this chapter, would not have done so without the principles of social action and self-directed groupwork. Joining together has given them the collective confidence and power they needed to speak out, attaining better services and to be better able to communicate with you. Hence, improving *your* service in the twenty-first century.

As Bob Holman, Community activist and author states clearly: people who use services *are* capable of planning and managing their own services. In October 2000, he wrote in the Guardian requesting that the Chancellor's £450m for preventative work should go directly to locally managed community groups. His fear is that we, as professionals and grant givers, do not trust ordinary people to organise themselves in an honest and efficient way. We therefore give the money to large national professional bodies and it never reaches the poor neighbourhoods (Guardian, 4.10.2000). Social workers could take a role in the community to facilitate this process. Ward mentions the many 'catch words' in social work: 'participation, citizenship and, sadly, empowerment', and suggests that these are in danger of becoming nothing more than 'meaningless, ideological deodorant' (1998: 36). Surely, in this century we can develop an approach to social work grounded in real empowerment, where service users take control, not just as our partners, but also as our managers.

We should not fear this transition, but have it as our central goal and the yardstick of our success. As a disabled friend told me, 'don't talk about involving us as service users, its up to us to decide whether we want to involve *you* as social workers'.

I began with an historical overview of the work, which encapsulated some of the major themes, which have located social work from the nineteenth to the twenty-first century. From citizens we can learn much about what social work should and should not be. Important themes centred upon hearing and learning from users, valuing their strengths, skills and aspirations, dispelling the myth of 'them and us', bringing humour to the work, raising confidence and political consciousness (our own and service user's) enabling people to join with others and take control of their lives and their services most importantly combatting racism and other forms of oppression. These are some of the core tenets of empowering social work practice. Now, the debate passes to you the newcomer (if such you are). Having heard a variety of views from within your own practice and from this text to emboss the profession with your own ideals and good practice. There is, then, no ultimate definition of social work. What counts as social work will depend on how powerful groups and institutions conceive of the role and tasks of social work – it is a contested concept – contested in and through a process of shaping and reshaping, as competing groups and interests vie for dominance in putting their own stamp on the profession (Thompson, 2000: 20). However, as Ahmad concludes, social work is not going to become anti-racist or even generally improved if:

> ...*social workers remain complacent and pretend that all is well...nor is it going to happen if social workers keep on waiting for their political masters and managers to hold their hands in paving their path for anti-racist social work...Social work action is dependent on social workers.*
>
> (Ahmad, 1993: 93)

Yours is the last word in this matter, to decide what social work can and should be in the twenty-first century, but the penultimate word falls to CP:

> *When I was six, I was taken into care by a social worker. When I was sixteen, I was asked to leave care and fend for myself by a social worker. Social workers were my parents. Some really cared for me as parents should, others were more interested in their careers, in pleasing their managers or paying their mortgage. As I got older, my relationship with social workers began to fall apart because I had my own mind. Kids get their own mind and fall out with mums and dads that way, but mums and dads always stick by you, no matter what. That's what social workers should do.*
>
> (CP, Member of YIPPEE, 2001)

Chapter 2

Social Work with Children and Families

Peter Nelson

Introduction

Social work with children and families reflects a fundamental tension between family support and child protection, between preventing child maltreatment and intervening to ensure child safety. This tension is present in legislation, governmental guidance, agency policy and individual practice. The resolution of that tension, whether it be at policy level and the way services are designed and delivered, or within an individual social worker's practice, is what shapes the services children and families receive. This chapter will explore the competing demands of family support and child protection and the effects that competition has on the social work services provided to children and families.

Setting the Context

'Why did no one try to save this bright, happy girl?'
(The Observer, 14 January 2001)

'We must now put into place stronger systems to protect children in the future.'
John Hutton, Health Minister, (Community Care, 18–24 January 2001)

Banner headlines in *The Observer* newspaper reported the death, in appalling circumstances, of Victoria Climbié, an eight-year-old girl, at the hands of her Aunt and Aunt's boyfriend. Alongside the headlines were the names of 'other lost children failed by the system: Maria Colwell – 1973, Jasmine Beckford – 1984, and Kimberley Carlile – 1987'. To those names could be added many others, in that there have been thirty-six inquiries into child deaths since Graham Bagnall was killed in Shropshire in 1973. In announcing the inquiry into Victoria Climbié's death, the health minister promised a 'root and branch reform' of child protection procedures if that is the only way to prevent another child dying in the same way.

The recent history of social work with children and families can be seen as very much a product of this process. That is a succession of well publicised child deaths, which have lead to: public inquiries each critical of social work practice, particularly the lack of social work intervention to safeguard children; and subsequent policy changes and practice guidance, which strengthens the emphasis on child protection.

A significant factor in this process is the role played by the media and its use of alarmist banner headlines. Thoburn (2001) has argued that it is not research or consumer feedback, which has led to policy change but rather individual cases in the headlines, headlines that are almost universally critical of social work competence (Franklin, 1999). Social workers are seen as failing to protect children and those failings are taken to be the result of the interaction of policy, practice and systems operating at a particular time (Parton, 2002). The focus of the often vehement criticism is that social workers fail to intervene in families with sufficient authority to protect children adequately. For example, the social worker in the Climbié case is described as 'naive beyond belief' in her contact with the child's carers and in not taking early action to remove the child. The subsequent inquiry recommendations have tended to stress the need for social workers: to be more assertive in their use of legislation to intervene in families to protect children, the need for improved working with other professionals and to have a greater knowledge of child abuse (Parton, 2002).

Ferguson has pointed out that the key premise of inquiries into child death, that it is possible for social work intervention to protect all children from abuse and death, is 'dangerously simplistic and in fact quite new' (Ferguson, 2002). He identifies 13,613 children as having died in child protection cases under scrutiny from the beginnings of the child protection movement in the late nineteenth century until 1914. The NSPCC originally published statistics on the deaths to show they were successfully reaching children at risk. This disclosure came to an end in the 1930s when it was seen to threaten the authority of and trust in the child protection system (Ferguson, 1997). It was, however, only in the 1970s, following the public inquiry into the death of Maria Colwell, that failure in the child protection system was blamed for such deaths and 'such failures became a shameful thing' (Ferguson, 2002).

Alongside these inquiries, however, has been the Cleveland inquiry (Secretary of State for Social Services, 1988) into the removal within a few weeks of over 100 children suspected of being sexually abused. The findings here were that social workers, alongside paediatricians, were over zealous in their intervention and failed to recognise the rights of parents in their rush to protect children. These findings had a major impact on the shape of the Children Act 1989, not only in terms of enshrining individual rights within legislation, but also in giving a greater role to the courts and lawyers in decision making in cases of suspected child abuse. The Children Act can be seen as placing child protection as one response within a wider range of services to children in need.

During the 1990s, a series of influential research programmes were carried out to examine whether social workers had the right balance between child protection and family support. (Department of Health, 1995; Audit Commission, 1994) The conclusion was that the balance was 'unsatisfactory', with social workers prioritising child protection investigations into suspected child abuse rather than preventative work, and not following up interventions with much needed family support. *Messages from Research*, published by the Department of Health (2000), emphasised the concept of emotional neglect, and that rather than a single abusive incident which tended to be the focus of social work investigation, long term harm to children was more likely to occur as a result of living in an environment which was 'low in warmth and high in criticism'. The result was that the needs of children and families were not being met. Social work services were urged to 'refocus' on family support. Government guidance asked social workers to assess the needs of children and their families rather than overly concentrating on the risk of potential harm (Department of Health, 2000).

One consequence of these conflicting demands is that social workers can be seen to be 'dammed if they do and dammed if they don't'. Within a culture that puts a heavy emphasis on individual blame, social workers are at fault if they do not remove a child who is at risk of harm but also at fault for unnecessary interventions in family life. They are at fault for emphasising investigations into children at risk, rather than providing resources to meet need, but at fault if a child is harmed. These tensions have an effect not only on the way services are delivered but also on the way social workers are perceived by themselves and others.

The influence a child protection paradigm has over the expectations of the community, in respect of social work with children and families, tends to be made clear to individual social workers during the initial stages of virtually any social work assessment. In the author's experience, irrespective of the nature of the assessment, the question is inevitably asked; 'You are not going to take my children away are you?' As Stevenson (1999: 88) argues, 'social workers are not seen as community friends'. This is the price they have paid for the increasing emphasis on the legal responsibility to protect children. In practice, working relationships between statutory social workers and the police, or social workers and local authority solicitors, tend to be stronger than those between social workers and therapeutic services (Harris, 1995). Parton (2002) sees these developments as a shift from understanding child abuse as essentially a medico-social problem where the doctor's expertise was prominent, to a socio-legal problem where lawyers take centre stage. The social work role has been reconfigured from one of diagnosing and preventing child abuse to investigating and assessing forensic evidence (Parton, 2002: 11; Home Office, 1992).

The concept of a paradigm is perhaps helpful in understanding the dominance child protection work has over social work with children and families (Hollows, 2001). Taken from the work of Kuhn (1970) in understanding how change occurs in the history of science, a paradigm is used to describe innovations that define the problems and methods of a research field for succeeding generations of practitioners. Change according to Kuhn occurs not by evolution but by revolution, by a paradigm shift, and it is change of this nature, which is required to refocus social work services away from child protection to family support – a shift to a new paradigm. Arguably, however, this is a shift that has never been made completely. As a result the tensions between the two competing paradigms of *child protection* and *family support* dominate both the organisation of social work services and individual practice.

The tension between these two paradigms can manifest itself in surprising ways. The 'New Labour' government, elected in 1997, has attempted to widen the refocusing debate beyond child protection and family support through expressing a commitment to: end child poverty; tackle social exclusion; and promote the welfare of all children (Department of Health, 2000). This is a corporate responsibility that extends beyond social work per se to include all local authorities, health authorities and community services. A number of programmes such as Sure Start and Connexions have been developed to promote policies aimed at early intervention, which support families, promote education and training and reduce truancy and school exclusion. Many of these programmes employ social work trained practitioners but the government emphasis is on social care personnel not social workers. Perhaps there is evidence of a distancing of 'New Labour' from the commonly perceived stigma and unpopularity of social workers. In addition, there is an impact on social services departments, as the primary provider of social work services to children and families. Encouraged through government policy initiates, to provide increasing levels of services to children in need, at the same time as socio-economic changes are increasing the numbers of such children, social services have been faced with considerable difficulties in respect of the planning and targeting of resources (Spratt, 2001). Social service departments struggle to find the capacity to meet the needs of families who require support primarily because of poverty (Tunstill, 1997). It is in this context that social services find themselves criticised by government, media and public when a failure in the child protection system occurs. These perceived failures may occur for a variety of complex and multi-faceted reasons. However, the emphasis tends to be on 'system' failure and the need to put in place new systems to prevent what is arguably never totally preventable. Once again, in organising services, as in individual practice, social work is 'damned if it does and dammed if it doesn't', pulled by the tensions of two competing paradigms.

In the light of such public criticism, it is perhaps not surprising that in terms of the services received by children and families it appears that the competition between paradigms is still dominated by child protection. Research by Spratt has identified that attempts to refocus social work on family support has been 'hampered by professional and organisational concern to manage risk' (Spratt, 2001: 933). Examining the services received by families referred for help with problems that at initial assessment did not need a child protection focus, he found that the identification and elimination of risk, rather than assessment and meeting of need, was the focus of social work intervention. Although the majority of social workers expressed a desire to move towards a family support approach, the management of risk and protecting children from harm dominated their actual practice. Spratt argues that one factor which works against refocusing social work practice is a culture of blaming individual practitioners for perceived practice mistakes, with the adoption of a safety first approach on the part of social workers (Spratt, 2001: 949).

Consequently, it could be argued that social work practice, with its dominant child protection paradigm, flies in the face of what everyone who is involved in social work with children and families knows. Services are overwhelmingly provided to children and families who are in poverty and who are experiencing the harmful effects of that poverty. The links between poverty and the chances that children will fail to thrive are well documented and researched (Utting, 1995; Hills, 1995): as are the implications for social work practice (Jack, 2000; Stevenson, 1997). There are clear links between inequality and increased mortality rates, deprivation and educational achievement, and poverty and rates of recorded child maltreatment and crime (Jack, 2000: 705). Children growing up in poverty have an increased likelihood of low income in adulthood, and there appears to be a strong intergenerational transmission of poverty (Department for Work and Pensions, 2002).

The Joseph Rowntree Inquiry (Hills, 1995) into the distribution of income and wealth in the UK found that children comprise 30 per cent of the poorest ten per cent of the population. The proportion of children living in relative poverty has increased threefold since 1980 and almost a third of children come from homes below the EU poverty line (Waterhouse and McGhee, 2002). Within developed countries, only New Zealand has experienced a faster growth in income inequality than the UK. By the mid-1990s, the UK had one of the highest proportions of children living in low-income households among developed countries (Department for Work and Pensions, 2002). Low income is a key aspect of child poverty in that it influences outcomes not only in childhood but also into adulthood.

Acknowledgement of the impact of poverty is present in social work evaluation and research, (Department of Health, 2001), and the introduction of policy initiatives and government guidance. For example the '*Framework for the Assessment of Children in Need and their Families*' (Department of Health, 2000: 1) which currently forms the basis for how children and families are initially assessed for social work services, begins with the statement that of approximately eleven million children in England over four million are living in poverty. Similarly, in considering the future development of services in the light of the Climbié inquiry, a partnership of the Local Government Association, Social Service Directors and the NHS Confederation graphically and succinctly describe the context for children and families social work:

- One in three children lives in poverty.
- One in four children lives in poor housing.
- 400,000 children in need live in England in 2000 – a ten per cent increase since 1999.

- Three out of five children in every classroom have witnessed domestic violence.
- More than one in three 12–15 year olds are assaulted each year.
- In 1999 12 per cent of 11–15 year olds had used drugs in the previous year.
- One in ten children have mental health problems.
- Infant mortality is twice as high for unskilled workers as for professional families.
- Afro Caribbean children are five times more likely to be excluded from school but no more likely to truant.

(ADSS, 2002; LGA, 2002)

It would appear, however, that to date, knowing these facts has not been sufficient to shift the paradigm in social work with children and families from child protection to family support.

Providing Services

Social work services to children and families are provided from a variety of sources including voluntary organisations such as NSPCC, Barnardo's and the growing number of programmes developed by 'New Labour' such as *Sure Start*. The primary source remains, however, the local authority social service department. The way such services are organised varies, and it is a recurring theme of such departments to reorganise their services with some frequency, both in response to dwindling resources and also government guidance. The basic structure tends to remain however, one of area based fieldwork teams, which may be subdivided into teams working primarily with initial referrals and assessment and those working with people over a longer term, such as, undertaking care proceedings and supporting looked after children. These area teams are supported by a range of specialist teams such as family placement dealing with fostering and adoption, and by day care and residential services.

Social workers within the area based teams have been described as the 'general practitioners' of the child welfare system, and employed in a range of activities including assessment, care planning and direct therapeutic work with children and families (Thoburn, 1996; Tunstill, 2000). Increasingly, however, social workers in those teams would find this description of themselves hard to recognise. As Jones, (2001) has identified, through a series of interviews with front line social workers, the day to day job has become one of undertaking child protection investigations and taking care proceedings. This is not a role that social workers appear to relish and the current recruitment crisis in social work perhaps reflects this reality (Jones, 2001)[1]. Direct

---

[1] The change to an undergraduate degree as the most usual form of professional qualification for new entrants has resulted in an increase in the numbers applying to study social work.

therapeutic work tends to be passed to specialist teams, as does family support, increasingly a generic term to describe anything other than child protection work.

It was not meant to be this way. Social work with children and families is currently shaped by legislation, in the form of the Children Act 1989; government guidance in the form of 'Working Together to Safeguard Children' (Department of Health, 1999); the 'Framework for the Assessment of Children in Need and their Families' (Department of Health, 2000); and the government's 'Quality Protects' initiative (Department of Health, 1998). Together these paint quite a different picture of what social work with children and families might be.

The Children Act 1989

Although the Children Act 1989 was not entirely a product of the Cleveland affair and child abuse inquiries, it did attempt to address the failures of the child welfare system. These are helpfully summarised by Tunstill (2000: 63) as the inadequate protection of children by social workers; over heavy interventions when they did intervene; the failure by social workers to offer support to parents; the stigmatisation of those who received support; and the tendency for parents to lose contact with children placed in care. The act provides the foundation for all social work interventions with children and families. It is based on a series of principles, which stress that the interests of most children are best served by being brought up by their own families. Consequently, participation and partnership, negotiation and agreement, with children and families, became key principles. The only way social workers could intervene against a families wishes was through the courts and on the basis that the child was suffering or likely to suffer significant harm (Tunstill, 2000).

In terms of current social work practice there are perhaps three sections of the Act containing concepts, which drive social work activities:

Part III of the Act places an obligation on the state to assist families who need help in bringing up their own children.

§17(1) states:
It shall be the general duty of every local authority –
- To safeguard and promote the welfare of children within their area who are in need; and
- So far as is consistent with that duty, to promote the upbringing of such children by their families, by providing a range of services appropriate to those children's needs.

§17(10) states:
A child shall be taken to be in need if –
a. he is unlikely to achieve or maintain or to have the opportunity of achieving or maintaining, a reasonable standard of health or development without the provision for him of services by his local authority

b. his health or development is likely to be significantly impaired, or further impaired, without the provision for him of such services; or
c. he is disabled.

Here there is a clear emphasis upon the notion that services should not be restricted to children who are at risk of abuse. In terms of practice, particularly during the 1990s, 'section 17' of the Act became synonymous with income maintenance. Paying 'section 17' money became a way of supporting families in poverty who had quite simply run out of money. In fact, section 17(6) defines services to include 'assistance in kind or, in exceptional circumstances, in cash.' Payment, often at the rate of £2 per day per child, became a way of tiding families over until their next benefit cheque. In this respect, section 17 was used in the same way as section 1 of the Child Care Act 1980 had been used previously. Here local authorities were under a duty to provide 'advice, guidance and assistance', which in 'exceptional' circumstances could include cash payments, to promote child welfare by diminishing the need to receive children into care. The test of whether paying sums of money would prevent reception into care has been carried over by some authorities into their interpretation of section 17 of the Children Act. In particular, interpretations of need have continued to be linked to an eligibility criteria based on risk (Department of Health, 2001). Any wider use of this section of the Act tended to be lacking, as energies and resources were taken up by Part V of the act and in particular, the requirement imposed by section 47.

§ 47(1) states:
Where a local authority –
a. are informed that a child who lives, or is found in their area –
    1. is the subject of an emergency protection order
    2. is in police protection; or
b. have reasonable cause to suspect that a child who lives, or is found in their area is suffering or likely to suffer, significant harm,
c. the authority shall make, or cause to make, such enquiries as they consider necessary to enable them to decide whether they should take action to safeguard or promote the child's welfare.

Significant harm is defined in section 31 of Part IV of the Act as *harm that can be equal with ill treatment (including sexual and non-physical abuse) or impairment of health (physical or mental) or development.*

'Significant', in relation to health or development, is defined as in comparison to what could reasonably be expected of a similar child. Where a child is found to be suffering or likely to suffer significant harm, and the harm is attributable to the care given not being what it would be reasonable to expect a parent to give, then there are grounds for the application for a care or supervision order.

In practice 'going out on a section 47', in order to assess the risk of significant harm and make judgements as to whether there are grounds for a care order has become a major part of the local authority social work role. The principles enshrined in the Children Act of partnership, participation and prevention have become dominated by risk assessments. As research by Beckett (2001) has demonstrated, the increase in numbers of risk assessment, led to an 'explosion' in the number of care proceedings. According to Beckett (2001, p 498) the Children Act was followed by a dramatic increase in the number of care proceedings: from 2,657 care order applications in 1992 to 6,728 in 1998. He goes on to suggest that contrary to expectations, the Children Act has:

> *...produced a shift in the balance of activities of social work agencies in the opposite direction to that intended: away from preventative services and towards those functions which social workers still refer to as 'statutory work', which is to say the functions that involve compulsion.*
>
> (Beckett, 2001: 498)

Beckett's research is supported by a number of studies, (Department of Health, 1994; Audit Commission, 1994; Aldgate and Tunstill, 1995), all of which acknowledge the dominance of a social policing role in social work practice and a priority of services to children at risk of significant harm over children in need. Having grown out of the tensions between child protection and family support, the Children Act and practice subsequent to the Act appears to reassert the pre-eminence of the child protection paradigm.

Quality Protects

Child protection work may well have retained its dominance, but throughout the 1990s, there were concerns about the quality of social work practice, both in terms of providing services and in protecting children. Mounting evidence was provided by Social Service Inspectorate Reports, evidence of children continuing to suffer serious abuse, and growing concerns over the system of public care for children (Mitchell, 2000). As part of the government's modernisation agenda the 'Quality Protects' (Department of Health, 1998) initiative was introduced to redress these shortfalls through the introduction of performance targets for local authorities:

- Increasing placement choice for looked after children.
- Establishing arrangements for listening to children.
- Developing management information systems.
- Improving assessment, care planning and record keeping.
- Developing effective quality assurance systems.
- Increasing support for children leaving public care.

(Mitchell, 2000: 191; Department of Health, 1998)

In terms of individual social work practice, some of these targets could seem rather remote. However, where major changes that affected practice did occur was in mechanisms to improve assessment through the introduction of the *Framework for the Assessment of Children in Need and their Families.*

Framework for the Assessment of Children in Need and their Families (Department of Health, 2000)

The Needs Assessment Framework was issued in 2000 under §7 of the Local Authority Social Service Act 1970, which requires local authorities to act under the general guidance of the secretary of state. As such, it does not have the full force of statute, but should be complied with unless local circumstances justify a variation. This guidance forms a key part of the 'Quality Protects Programme' and the wider governmental programme to tackle social exclusion. Introduced to encourage early intervention to support children and families and promote integrated working among local agencies, for example: health, education and social services alongside voluntary and private agencies, the guidance is intended to be used by those involved in undertaking assessments of children in need and their families under the Children Act 1989 (Department of Health, 2000). As such, the framework re-introduces the concept of *children in need* into mainstream social work with children and families, and tries to place this notion – and all that it implies – at the forefront of social work activity.

The basis of social work activity is assessment and there is some evidence that it has not been one of the strengths of social work practice (Adcock, 2002). In particular, practice has concentrated on the gathering of information at the expense of analysis, judgement and decision-making. In addition, social workers have concentrated on assessing the risk of significant harm to the detriment of assessment of need (Rose, 2000). The Department of Health guidance aims to provide a framework for assessing or understanding what is happening to a child through considering the interactions of three systems or domains: namely:

- a child's developmental needs;
- the parenting capacity to respond to those needs;
- the wider family and environmental factors.

(Rose, 2000)

The intention is not only to collect information but also to provide a coherent means of analysing information gathered, in order to decide how best to safeguard and promote a child's welfare.

Based upon wide ranging research findings, the underpinning principles of the framework can be seen as providing a summary of the aims and aspirations of a new orthodoxy in social work practice. For example assessments:

- Are child centred.
- Are rooted in child development.

- Are ecological in their approach.
- Ensure equality of opportunity.
- Involve working with children and families.
- Build on strengths as well as identify difficulties.
- Are inter-agency in their approach to assessment and the provision of services.
- Are a continuing process not a single event.
- Are carried out in parallel with other action in providing services.
- Are grounded in evidence based knowledge.

(Department of Health, 2000: 10)

In setting out these principles, the framework provides indicators for good social work practice and in addition indicates a change of direction in two significant areas. Firstly, effective social work practice is linked to an analysis of poverty through the ecological approach, where family context and culture are as important as the child–parent relationship (Jack, 2000). Secondly, the framework makes virtually no mention of the concept of risk or the assessment of risk. Rather the focus is on need, and the concept of significant harm is made subservient to one of need, in that 'some children are in need because they are suffering or likely to suffer significant harm' (Department of Health, 2000a: 7). Consequently, the framework can be seen as reasserting the principles of the Children Act 1989 and providing a direct challenge to the child protection paradigm.

Working Together to Safeguard Children (Department of Health, 1999)

Where children are in need because they are suffering or likely to suffer significant harm, the local authority is obliged by section 47 of the Children Act to consider initiating enquiries to find out what is happening to the child and whether action should be taken to protect the child. In describing this process, the Needs Assessment Framework (Department of Health, 2000: 8) carefully states that this 'implies the need to assess what is happening to a child', rather than an assessment of the risk to the child of significant harm. The procedures which govern these enquiries are laid down in 'Working Together to Safeguard Children' (Department of Health, 1999).

These procedures provide a guide to inter-agency working which both 'safeguard' and 'promote the welfare' of children. The assessment must focus on any harm that may have occurred to the child as a result of child maltreatment, but establishing the extent and nature of that harm is not of itself sufficient. The assessment should also be developed to inform plans and services, which may be required to promote and safeguard the child's welfare. In this respect 'Working Together to Safeguard Children' (1999: 2) clearly states that effective measures to safeguard children should not be seen in isolation from family support services. The guidance states the importance of maintaining a clear focus on the welfare of the child, but in doing so:

> *Just as child protection processes should always consider the wider needs of the child and family, so broad-based family support services should always be alert to, and know how to respond quickly and decisively to potential indicators of abuse and neglect.*

(Department of Health, 1999: 2)

It is perhaps this multi-focal way of viewing social work with children and families, that both in terms of organisation of services and also, in respect of individual practice, proves so elusive. Consequently, it is the tension between child protection and family support rather than the synthesis of the two, which has tended to dominate social work practice.

Family Support

Legislation, government guidance, social workers, and children and families themselves all express a wish to refocus social work with children and families towards family support. Yet, such is the dominance of the child protection paradigm that family support tends to be discussed only in respect of the extent to which it is a reaction to child protection. Family support is everything else other than child protection. There is a clear hierarchy in terms of research, staff training and expertise, and allocation of resources on an agency or individual basis. Child protection comes first and rarely is family support explored, discussed and refined in its own right.

The Audit Commission's definition (Audit Commission, 1994) reflects that generality when it defines family support as:

> *Any activity or facility either provided by statutory agencies or by community groups and individuals, aimed at providing advice, and support to parents to help them in bringing up children.*

(Audit Commission, 1994: 192)

There are, however, other attempts to understand the concept (Hollows, 2002). For example, Hearn (1995) defines family support in terms of imput and outcome; for example, how activities and networks alleviate stress and promote parental competence. Other definitions tend to reflect the polarity with child protection. For example, MacLeod and Nelson (2000) identify family support with promoting 'family wellness' as distinct from preventing child maltreatment, where the fundamental difference is whether services are proactive or reactive, whether they promote well-being or react to alleged maltreatment.

The meaning of family support in practice is usefully explored in a study by Tunstill and Aldgate (2000), which looked at the needs of families, and the support they were offered, following referral to social services for services under section 17 of the Children Act (rather than referral for child protection reasons). This study identified a sample of families who had been struggling for a long time before asking for help, but for whom social services was the first port of call when help was requested. The families requested and obtained services in respect of stress relief, help with child development, improved family relationships and alleviation of practical problems. A third of the families, however, received no help and those families in need because of social deprivation were least likely to obtain a service. The most requested form of help, social work support, or what has traditionally been described as 'casework', namely listening, sharing problems and advocacy, as distinct form providing material resources, was least likely to be met (Tunstill and Aldgate, 2001: 236).

Challenges for the Future

There are perhaps three issues identified by Tunstill and Aldgate, which are significant, not only for the provision of family support, but also for the present and future provision of children and families social work as a whole. Firstly, the fact that although the link between poverty and poor outcomes for children is well established, this has yet to be translated into social work practice. Secondly, the notion of a threshold of eligibility, in that once a family got through this threshold a range of services was available, has been widely applied; yet for a third of families in the study, the threshold was set too high and consequently they did not receive a service. Thirdly, the acknowledgement by social workers that the type of social work (i.e. 'casework') requested by families was important but 'they were often unable to offer it because of the expectation that they focus on child protection' (Tunstill and Aldgate, 2001: 237).

Spratt (2001: 952) has identified the 'need to manage risk' as the pervasive influence on all social work intervention, both in terms of the organisation of services and crucially at the level of individual practice, irrespective of whether the referral concerns child protection or some other need for children and families. In explaining why this might be the case the work of Dalgleish (2000) is perhaps useful. In considering assessment and decision making in respect of risk and needs assessment he usefully explores the influence of personal thresholds, and concludes that 'thresholds are influenced not by the case information but by the values placed on the consequences by the decision maker' (Dalgleish, 2000: 16). It may be that the values held, and thresholds set by individual social work practitioners, require exploration in understanding the failure to achieve the paradigm shift expected by legislation and guidance.

The introduction by the Prime Minister, Tony Blair, to the Green Paper 'Every Child Matters' (Department for Education and Skills, 2003) locates the proposals for future services for children clearly within the tension of competing paradigms.

'People, practices and policies' are to be put in place to make sure that 'risk is as small as is humanly possible' but reducing risk is not sufficient and it is also necessary to maximise children's opportunities, 'to improve their life chances, to change the odds in their favour'. Written in large measure as a response to Lord Laming's report into the death of Victoria Climbié (Department of Health, 2003), it is no surprise that issues of child protection are central. However, Laming made clear in his recommendations, that child protection could not be separated from policies to improve children's lives as a whole. Consequently, the Green Paper seeks to 'both protect children and maximise their potential' (Department for Education and Skills, 2003: 5).

The proposals in the Green Paper seek to bring together education and children's social services at a local and national level within a single organisation or Children's Trust. Professionals will be encouraged to work in multi-disciplinary teams based around schools or Children's Centres and under the control of a Director of Children's Services at local level, and a new Minister for Children, Young People and Families at national level. The proposals are grouped around four main areas:

- Supporting parents and carers.
- Early intervention and effective protection.
- Accountability and integration at a national and local level.
- Workforce reform.

In so doing, these proposals can be seen as reflecting the principles, if not the language, of the Children Act 1989 in seeking to focus on children in need and not only on children in need of protection. The challenge for the future will be to see if the proposals and resulting legislation can bring about the shift from a dominant child protection paradigm, which has so far eluded social work with children and families.

In considering future developments, the concept of a paradigm remains useful, in particular through understanding that social workers operate in a world, which is wider than that of professional guidance and agency policy. The influence of the media, public expectations, and well publicised child death inquiries strengthen the dominant child protection paradigm. The expectation of a shift in that paradigm brought about solely from a professional basis may be unrealistic. The tensions between child protection and family support, however, are played out at every level of social work practice. The issue therefore becomes one not of shifting from one approach to another but of achieving a balance, of moving from a polarisation of thinking and action to one which encompasses a range of interventions within the same family. The resolution of the tensions between family support and child protection, balanced or not, shapes the social work services received by children and families.

Chapter 3

Community Care For Older People

Cherry Rowlings

Part One: Exploring the Issues

Community care for older people shares many of the opportunities and problems, hopes and disappointments and, above all, tensions and conflicts of community care for any section of the population. This is not surprising, as community care, by its very nature, is contentious and contested territory, involving as it does views about the duties, rights and responsibilities of society as a whole towards its members, of families towards parents, partners, children and relatives, of neighbours for those who happen to live in the same street, of individuals for themselves and others. The extent to which there *is* community care, the way it is funded, who provides it and in what ways – all are expressions of the kind of contract that exists between the state and its citizens.

Community care for older people, however, is distinguished by several particular features. The most immediately evident is the size and scale of what is involved. In their report on *Social work in the Millennium*, the Association of Directors of Social Work (ADSW) in Scotland sum this up in their statement that 'the long term care for older people is perhaps the single most critical social problem for central Government at the present time' (ADSW, 1997: 43). Their use of the word 'problem' is not unusual in this context – a point that will be returned to later in this introductory section. For the moment, it is important to grasp the significance of numbers and of population structure. The following figures are based on pensionable age, which in Britain is presently sixty years for women and sixty-five years for men.

In the UK as a whole, around 18 per cent of the population is over pensionable age – compared to six per cent at the beginning of the twentieth century. Within this time span, numbers have increased from just over two million to around 10.5 million (OPCS, 1991). Many more people can therefore expect to live into old age, an achievement due largely to improvements in public health and in preventive medicine which have substantially reduced deaths in childbirth (of mother and of infant), in childhood (from diseases such as diphtheria, scarlet fever or measles) and in adulthood (for example from tuberculosis or pneumonia). Well over ninety per cent of older people live in the community although the proportion living in institutional care increases with greater age.

Greater longevity has been accompanied by falling birth rates (itself a contributing reason why the *proportion* of older people has increased so considerably) and this trend is predicted to continue. Taking Scotland as an example, a total population of 5.1 million in 1994 is expected to fall to 4.8 million in the year 2034. The number of children under 16 years, just over 1 million in 1994, is likely to be down to 824,000 in 2034. By contrast, the population over pensionable age is predicted to rise from 912,000 to 1.3 million, an increase of 50 per cent. By 2034, for every hundred people of working age in the population, there will be 51 over pensionable age, considerably higher than the comparable figure for children under 16, of whom there will be 31 for every hundred people of working age. Add these figures together and the enormity of the population change can be appreciated: in 2034, there will be 82 dependents for every hundred working people, compared with a combined figure of 61 in 1994 (The Scottish Office, 1996).

It is of course true that many older people, especially those recently retired and the gradually increasing number with occupational pensions, will make limited demands upon state services and will be active contributors to the economy and, indeed, to the provision of care for people older and sometimes younger than themselves. The more significant figures therefore relate to the group aged 75 or over, for it is the so called 'old old' who are more likely to need health and social care, whose informal support networks are usually less robust and whose reliance upon state provided services will be greater. The significance of being over 75 can be seen from a survey of older people in the community in England in 1991/92 (McCafferty, 1994). Whilst 52 per cent of those aged below 75 could be described as fully independent, for those aged 75 to 84 it was 33 per cent and for those over 85, 14 per cent.

Returning to the population in Scotland, which reflects the situation elsewhere in the UK, the most dramatic increase in numbers is within the 75 year and over age group – from 318,000 in 1994 to 543,000 in 2034 (The Scottish Office, 1996). It is the combination of the actual numbers with the rate and speed of the increase (by 71 per cent in the next 40 years) that is the prime reason why the Association of Directors of Social Work (referred to earlier) describes the long term care of older people as a policy 'problem' of such magnitude. It also explains why the development and implementation of community care, as both a social and an economic policy, has come to be so dominated by the needs of older people, even though as a concept it was articulated most clearly in earlier debates on improving services for people with mental health problems (see, for example, the Report of the Royal Commission on the Law Relating to Mental Illness and Mental Deficiency, 1957).

In their analysis of the implementation of the major legislative reform of community care, the National Health Service and Community Care Act, 1990, Lewis and Glennerster (1996) show how the driving force to promote community care on a scale hitherto unknown was the cost to central Government of residential and nursing home care for older people which, by the end of the 1980s, had become unsustainable. Due to an earlier change in regulations, older people eligible for State financial benefit to supplement a low retirement income could enter a private residential or nursing home without any assessment of need or any attempt to find cheaper community based alternatives – and central Government met the cost. Not surprisingly, private provision increased dramatically. In 1979, the cost to Government was £10 million. Within a few years, it was £500 million and by 1991, £200 million. As Lewis and Glennerster wrote:

What was new in the 1980s was the runaway cost of giving families what amounted to an open cheque to buy residential and nursing home care – the most expensive kind of [care] available. No government could have let such a situation continue. In the end, stopping it was the Conservative government's prime concern.

(Lewis and Glennerster, 1996: 193)

If the economic imperative was the strongest force, it is important to note it was not the only one. In respect of providing for older people in need of care and support, there were widespread and long-standing concerns about the poor quality of care, inflexible services, the absence of user choice and an over bureaucratic response to user need. Several studies had shown that the provision of care was too often a 'hit and miss' affair, dependent less on need and more on what services happened to be available. Health and social care provision was in many places poorly co-ordinated, resulting in gaps in some services and duplication of others (Audit Commission, 1986; Sinclair et al., 1990; Le Grand and Bartlett, 1993). Enquiries into abuse of residents by staff in old people's homes had revealed again the shortcomings of some residential establishments (Gibbs et al., 1987). Yet residential provision absorbed a significant proportion of local authority, expenditure on older people – to the detriment, some argued, of alternative forms of care, even though successive studies showed that, given a choice, most older people in need of care preferred to receive this in their own home rather than in a residential institution. There was therefore unease and frustration from a number of sources – voluntary groups representing older people, practitioners working in this field and managers responsible for service development. The need for change was not disputed and the necessity was provided by the economic factors previously described.

There are, however, other factors which also may be said to distinguish community care for older people from that provided for other groups in society. First of these is the significance of gender (Arber and Ginn, 1996). Both being old and being a carer of older people are experiences primarily of women. More than two thirds of people aged 75 years or over are women. When care is provided, it is primarily by women members of the family or by staff in statutory, voluntary or private organisations, who are also predominantly women. Although the contribution to caring by male carers (usually husbands caring for an ill or disabled wife) has been acknowledged (Arber and Ginn, 1991), caring and being cared for in old age are inextricably part of wider issues about the role and status of women in society and the nature of the expectations and responsibilities of one generation of women in respect of another (Hallett, 1989).

A second distinguishing feature of the elderly population is that is consists predominantly of people living alone or in a two person household (91 per cent). As people grow older, the more likely it is that they will be living alone: whereas 36 per cent of people aged 65 to 74 live alone, this rises to 68 per cent for those aged 85 and over. Significantly, older people living alone consume a greater amount of health and social care services – roughly two and a half times more per year than elderly couples (McCafferty, 1994). Thus, although Lewis and Glennerster (1996) noted above that the cost to the Government of funding residential care was a major incentive to develop community care alternatives, it can be seen that the funding of community care is also a major issue and one which in the next section will reappear in the discussion on the increasing use by local authorities of charging for social care services that used to be provided free for substantial numbers of older people.

A final distinguishing feature to be considered, in this section, is that old age is likely to affect all of us in some way and at some time. It has been argued that this is particularly important for the paid and unpaid carers of older people (Rowlings, 1981). In a very real sense, most carers are facing what could be their future when they provide support or care for an older person. Furthermore, many paid carers may at the same time be providing unpaid care to an elderly parent, relative or neighbour. The dynamics of caring are always complex but an added dimension to caring for older people is knowing and fearing that this is how life could be for me, my parent, spouse or partner in so many years time.

It is perhaps because of the wish to disassociate oneself from this distressing prospect that, traditionally, caring for older people has not been a popular area of professional practice for nurses, doctors or social workers. Within UK society as a whole, of course, older people are not a high status social group. Younger people have a far more negative and pessimistic view of old age as a time of life than older people themselves have. There is a tendency to depersonalise, to refer to 'the elderly' as if older people were a homogenous, undifferentiated group, despite the fact that people may live 30 years or more past retirement. As we saw in the *Report* from the Association of Directors of Social Work (ADSW, 1997), caring for older people is often referred to as a 'problem' and there is often talk of the 'burden' of an ageing population rather than pride in the achievement of successfully reducing premature mortality. A similar negativity is reflected in the way in which some English words associated with old age have acquired a pejorative meaning. The word 'geriatric' may be used as a term of abuse in a way that its child equivalent – 'paediatric' – would never be. The comment 'he or she is going senile' has come to be a dismissive shorthand for any cognitive impairment, illness, or even just unconventional behaviour in an older person. Professional carers are part of the society in which they work and we will see later in this chapter how their practice can be affected by ageist assumptions. Additionally, however, as has been suggested above, their work with ill or disabled older people faces them with what they fear might be their own future. No other aspect of care work can do that for so many and the implementation of community care will be influenced not just by carers' ability to challenge and overcome the ageism that is part of UK society but also by how comfortable they are with the prospect of their own ageing and possible need for care.

Part Two: Providing Community Care

The previous section sketched the political, social and economic context of providing care in the community for older people. Again, it must be stressed that it is a minority of older people who need such services. To reinforce this message, it is instructive to note that in the 1991/92 survey of older people in England referred to already (McCafferty, 1994), amongst those aged 75 and over and living alone, only 25 per cent had a home help, only 16 per cent were being visited by a community nurse and only nine per cent were receiving a domiciliary meals service. More commonly, therefore, people looked after themselves, with or without help from family or neighbours.

It is however, with the minority receiving services that this chapter is concerned. One of the consequences of the reforms introduced by the National Health Service and Community Care Act, 1990, and developed in implementation guidance from central Government, has been a fundamental change in the structures through which health and social care services are delivered. These will be outlined, albeit briefly, before closer examination of community care practice.

The 1990 Act introduced the principles of the market to the provision of hospital care and community based health and social services. This was achieved largely through imposing a separation between the purchase and the provision of services (the purchaser/provider split), even though in reality such a division was not always clear-cut. Additionally, the Act both increased and dramatically changed both the role and the responsibilities of the local authority in the provision of social care. Examples of the increase can be seen in the extended responsibility for the inspection of day and residential centres (subsequently to pass to national Commissions following devolution), in becoming the assessor for all long term care for adults where the state would be meeting some or all of the cost and in being the identified lead agency for community care planning and co-ordination. The change in their role was that they were required to shift from being the sole or major provider of formal care to being a purchaser in a 'market place' of services from the private and voluntary sectors as well as from their own (but often reducing) in-house staff. Local authorities were thus to 'enable' rather than to provide community care. In England and Wales (but not in Scotland), this enabling role was driven by a central Government requirement that 85 per cent of the extra money local authorities received to finance their new responsibilities had to be spent in the independent sector. Through this mechanism Government hoped that not only would more varied and flexible services be developed, thereby increasing consumer choice, but also that costs would be reduced by the competitive forces of the market. So, how have these changes affected community care for older people?

Experimental projects in England that provided intensive and co-ordinated community care for older people who would otherwise have needed residential care had shown, before the 1990 reforms, that it was possible to maintain in the community people with a high level of dependency. Moreover, there was considerable consumer satisfaction with the care received and the costs were less than providing residential care (Challis and Davies, 1986; Challis et al. 1990). These projects involved a case manager who assessed need, who held his or her own budget to purchase care from a variety of sources and who then assembled 'packages of care', drawing on the resources of volunteers, paid professional staff and family carers as available and appropriate. Careful assessment, in which the older person and his/her informal carers were fully involved, had enabled a level of user participation in defining need and identifying solutions that had not been typical of practice in community care. It was this model of service delivery that was promoted by Government guidance following the 1990 Act, although the language changed from 'case' management to 'care' management (Department of Health, 1991). In meeting need, there was to be a distinction between simple and complex. Whereas service users with 'simple' needs, such as for a straightforward bathing aid or help with the heavier aspects of housework, could just receive what was adjudged appropriate, those with 'complex' needs were to have a designated care manager to assemble a proper package of care. Thereafter, this care package was to be subject to monitoring and review, although there was less Government guidance on these activities than on the detail of proper assessment. Furthermore, assessment was to be of need and not just of eligibility for specific services; in the language of the guidance, it was to be 'needs led' and not a 'service led' activity. Attention to the needs of informal carers was also included in the reforms and was subsequently to be strengthened by further legislation (Carers (Recognition and Services) Act, 1995) which acknowledge their right to a separate assessment of their needs and circumstances. This does not necessarily mean they will then receive a service; as is the case for all potential recipients of community care, there is no right to services and in making decisions about what, if any resources to provide, social services departments are required to keep within their allocated budgets and to ration services as their budgets dictate.

However, as has already been noted, the projects that so influenced Government guidelines were experimental in nature – relatively small scale and involving trained staff with low caseloads. This was very different from what was now required as authorities began to grapple with their new and expanded responsibilities (Department of Health, 1994; Lewis and Glennerster, 1996; Petch et al., 1996). Moreover, they had to contend with cuts in their main budget and some also found that the additional money allocated by central Government to pay for the increased community care workload was considerably below what they needed. Hence, it is not surprising that the delivery of community care has become so bound up with the introduction or extension of charging for services provided. To quote Baldwin and Lunt (1996: 7), charging became a 'major policy issue in the 1990s' and their research illustrated the enormous variations between authorities in the amount service users were required to pay and in the way charges were calculated and levied.

Charging and its counterpart, the ability to pay for any or all of the services that may be provided, has had an impact on large numbers of older people, from those needing relatively simple help with housework or shopping to those reliant upon paid care to provide services essential for daily living. As local authorities have struggled to keep within their community care budgets, so charging has become an important source of additional income and at the same time, services have increasingly been targeted at those with the greatest need. Two consequences have followed. The first is that for many older people and their carers, an ability and willingness to pay may significantly influence the quality and the quantity of care received – perhaps paying completely for lower levels of need that would otherwise not be met, or contributing to the cost of a package of care or 'topping up' the service provided by the local authority. How many go without or accept a lower level of service or manage to pay the cost by reducing spending in other, possibly necessary areas of living is unknown. However, Baldwin and Lunt (1996) came across worrying evidence from social services staff to indicate that both the take-up and the continued use of services that older people had been assessed as needing have been adversely affected. The introduction of free personal care (in Scotland) and free nursing care (in England) has gone some way in alleviating the financial repercussions for older people and their families but low levels of care and ineligibility for service in the first place will both impose costs on individuals.

The second consequence of limited resources has been an increasing concentration upon service users with the higher levels of dependency. The result is that 'need has come to mean high dependency and high risk' (Lewis and Glennerster, 1996: 162). Lower levels of need may either not be recognised as such by social services staff or the older person is left to make their own arrangements on a private basis. The efforts of those deemed ineligible for service to 'keep going' have been described by Tanner (2001) and yet again point to the importance for well-being of so-called low level services such as gardening and house cleaning.

Her respondents also described the difficulties of being purchasers, even when they had the financial resources to pay for help. It has been argued that this exclusion of lower level needs reduces the opportunities for care management to take on a preventive role, thereby promoting a better quality of life for many older people and their carers and as a result, reducing the likelihood of crises in the informal care network at a later date when there is less chance of avoiding a total breakdown of care (Allen et al., 1992; Audit Commission, 1997; Fletcher, 1998). There must remain concerns about the impact of targeting, especially on those older people whose need is serious but not quite serious enough to lead to a properly developed care package.

Whatever the organisational context – and local authorities have always rationed community care services for older people, albeit less openly – the assessment of need amongst older people in itself poses particular challenges. Successive studies have shown that older people themselves tend to under report both health and social need (Goldberg et al., 1970; Isaacs and Neville, 1976; Levin et al., 1988). Perhaps this is because they have low expectations for their quality of life in old age or they are used to, even proud of, being independent and making the best of what they have. There is certainly some evidence that they may not report medical problems because they mistakenly attribute these to the ageing process. However, successive studies have shown that many do not ask for help because they do not know that help could be available (Tester and Meredith, 1987; Tanner, 2001; Richards, 2000). This is particularly likely to happen when the older person is a first generation immigrant and has limited knowledge of the English language (Cameron et al., 1996; Phillipson et al., 2001). Carers, too, may have a very good understanding of what help they need, but do not approach the social services department because they are unaware that a relevant service exists (Levin et al., 1988).

In these circumstances, the skill of the person carrying out the assessment becomes particularly important. Previous research has shown that social workers, and other professionals, have often had a narrow view of older people's needs and a pessimistic approach towards what could be done. Older people have been seen as having mainly practical problems for which straightforward services were all that was required (Goldberg and Warburton, 1978; DHSS, 1978; Rowlings, 1985). Social and emotional needs have therefore been ignored and sometimes physical needs too. It is an indictment of both the nursing and social work professions that some workers still have limited aspirations for older clients (SSI, 1997) and that the call is still being made for work with older people to be 'valued and promoted as a high status aspect of practice' (Nolan, 2000: 70).

If the rhetoric of community care is ever to be realised, a radical shift in practice is required, towards assessments that are more sensitive to and respectful of older people. This entails a focus on what people *can* do and not just on what they cannot, that takes account of their strengths and aspirations and does not concentrate only on deficits. It means that assessment must also be based on a fuller understanding of the older person as a person, what is important for them, how they spend their day and their night (managing periods of wakefulness in the night is a common feature of many older people's lives), what things they would like improved and how they think this could be achieved. An approach such as this includes the older person in the assessment and in what happens thereafter, rather than imposing what the worker thinks is best. It increases the chances that where help is needed, it will 'fit' with the person's existing ways of managing and with the other support networks that are involved. Sensitive, integrated and non-discriminatory care are amongst the aims of the Government's National Service Framework (NSF) for the Care of Older People, the development of which is described by Philp et al. (2000). It remains to be seen whether and how far this policy initiative can achieve consistent and high standards of care. (Note the NSF is not UK wide and does not, for example, apply in Scotland.)

The research on case management in the 1980s showed how vital personalised assessment was to successful outcomes of care (Challis and Davies, 1986). In addition, this research highlighted the importance of attending to the *maintenance* of any care package assembled. This was, in part, to monitor the appropriateness of what was being provided (the circumstances of the older person or of someone in the care network can change very quickly) but also to provide support to those providing the care. This is an acknowledgement that being cared for and providing care has a dynamic, which can at times be stressful, or a source of conflict. Moreover, the continued presence of the case manager, albeit often in the background, was evidence to carers, both paid and unpaid, that they had not been left alone with all the responsibility. This is an important point. Carers in the community are often isolated; they may work in an older person's house on their own and they do not have the kind of contacts and support as do, for example, care staff in residential homes. Yet, the nature of their work may be very similar. As people with higher levels of dependency are being helped in the community, so carers are working in the context of heightened risk and it is appropriate that responsibilities should be shared.

However, it was suggested previously that far more attention has been focused on how to carry out assessments following the 1990 Act than on how to manage care, once an assessment has been made. Two studies in Scotland, separated by six years, exemplify the issues, which, for example, the Social Services Inspectorate (1997) found in England. First, Petch et al. (1996), studied four Scottish local authorities and showed that neither monitoring nor review were regular and routine activities. It was not always clear who was undertaking the monitoring that did happen, nor what exactly their responsibilities were. Frequently, monitoring was undertaken by the providers of services and not by the purchasers. This could mean that although each aspect of service provision was monitored, no one was looking at the care package as a whole. Second, Stalker and Campbell (2002) concluded from their interviews in all thirty-two local authorities that there appeared to be a lack of clarity surrounding not the aims of monitoring and review but how and when they should be carried out, with perhaps too much monitoring and too little reviewing taking place. They found variations in the frequency of reviews, whether all or only some cases were reviewed and who actually conducted the review. With regard to monitoring, care managers described more involvement (mostly through home visits and telephone calls) than their seniors thought was happening and there was also a discrepancy between the two groups as to who was responsible for monitoring. This prompted the comment from the researchers that 'if all those identified were actually doing it, then a disproportionate amount of time and effort is being spent on monitoring' (Stalker and Campbell, 2002: 53).

This gap in the management of care assumes a greater significance when it is remembered that purchasing community care services for older people on such a scale is still a relatively new activity for local authorities. In some instances, purchasing will be an individual decision, with a specific older person in mind and therefore tailored closely to his or her particularly needs and circumstances. But in other cases, probably the majority, the care manager will have made use of services provided by one or more independent agencies who have signed a block contract with the social services department to provide, say, cleaning or personal care. It might be that the independent agency cannot provide the most appropriate services for that older person, but the care manager cannot purchase alternatives because of the centrally negotiated contract and because benefits are not devolved to care manager level (Stalker and Campbell, 2002), thus user choice may be eroded. Yet the dilemma facing the local authority is a difficult one: older people with high dependency needs must be assured of regular and reliable services. A block contract of a year or more offers greater security of provision than is available through purchasing single, one-off services as and when need arises. It may also be cheaper because the independent agency has a guaranteed income over time and the local authority has a greater chance of achieving better quality because of the on-going commitment between it and the agency. However, as already suggested, these undoubted benefits may mean that the care manager has less flexibility and fewer opportunities to assemble individually tailored care packages. How purchasing decisions are made and what the outcomes are for the service user, informal carers and paid workers are aspects of community care for older people that must not get lost in the wider debates about the overall level of resources, what constitutes need and who should pay for services.

Part Three: Challenges for the Future

This chapter concludes with some further key issues for community care for older people over the next five years or so.

The first has a familiar ring to it – namely, who should receive care management and who should provide it? Stalker and Campbell's (2002) study of care management in Scotland shows continuing diversity and uncertainty across local authorities. The early case management projects referred to in Part Two of this chapter and the care management guidance of the early 1990s had identified complex, higher dependency and higher risk situations as requiring care management, as distinct from those where simpler, more straightforward advice or services were required. The distinction between 'simple' and 'complex' were variously employed in the Scottish authorities, leading the researchers to conclude that 'clearer differentiation' was needed in respect of levels of assessment, the 'frequency and form of monitoring and review' and the deployment of qualified and unqualified staff. These are important points, indicating that in the decade or so of its existence within community care, care management has yet to achieve consistency in implementation in at least one part of the UK. It would not be surprising to find that these situations were replicated in other countries within the United Kingdom.

A related point is the extent to which care management and the tasks of assessment, monitoring and review, are focused upon the services necessary for physical survival. The discourse of care management does not give prominence to social and emotional needs, although it can of course be argued that good and reliable physical care has a positive impact on personal well-being and will often contribute to improved relationships with informal carers. However, therapeutic work with social or emotional problems has to be recognised as an appropriate part of (some) interventions. To take one, not very well publicised area: many of today's older people had unhappy wartime (World War Two) experiences, – as prisoners of war, as victims of civilian bombing, as members of the military. Some will have witnessed terrible events, some will even have perpetrated terrible things. In old age, they may find that their ability to keep these memories and images in the background has weakened. As a result, past trauma becomes a powerful and disabling factor in their present life, although they and others may be unaware of the link between present anxiety, depression or bizarre behaviour and the terrifying experiences of the past. Therapeutic intervention is possible and can be successful, but only if professionals are able to bring their counselling, groupwork or care skills to older people (Hunt et al., 1997).

Two other groups of older service users require a similar sensitivity to their needs. The first is older people from minority ethnic groups, who were immigrants as younger people and who have grown old and can expect to die and be buried or have their ashes scattered in a land other than their country of origin. Some may still have a limited knowledge of English, many will find that services have been developed with the indigenous British population in mind and that sensitivity to different cultural or religious norms is limited (Blakemore and Boneham, 1994). Yet things such as the food, clothes and religious rituals of one's childhood may become essential reminders of identity in old age, especially if a person has dementia or has outlived others of their own generation (Myerhoff, 1979). Too often, the majority population makes assumptions about people in minority groups; a common one that still persists in the UK, despite evidence to the contrary, is that all older people from black or minority ethnic groups will be looked after by their family and so there is no need to develop ethnically sensitive practice and services. The combination of this misunderstanding and of limited appropriate services can impose excessive demands upon family units and deprive people of access to services available to the majority population (Phillipson et al., 2001; Chan and Yu, 2000). Here, above all, the assessment skills outlined in the previous section have a vital place in the provision of community care for older people.

The other group of older people that may similarly face insensitivity to their needs are people with dementia. Here, too, myths abound, and again these seem to aim to reassure the rest of the population. Thus it may be said 'she doesn't know what time of day it is, so it doesn't matter what you do' or 'he's too demented to notice what is happening'. As understanding of dementia increases, so we are better able to relate to people with dementia as people and not as 'the demented' and to listen to what they have to tell us about themselves and what their likes and dislikes are (Goldsmith, 1996; Kitwood, 1997). Nevertheless, practice skills are still undeveloped in this area and the resulting insensitivities may well exacerbate the older person's difficulties rather than bring about some improvement.

The next five years are likely to see an increased concern over abuse of older people, by their families and by paid carers. The incidence of abuse in the UK has proved difficult to estimate with any reliability. Definitions of abuse are also hard to pin down, though most people would include physical ill treatment, financial abuse in the form of misuse of the older person's money or possessions, medical abuse (withholding or excessive use of medication), sexual abuse and emotional abuse (screaming, shouting and offensive remarks). There are real anxieties that as services become more limited, so families will be less supported and relationships put under greater strain. We are a long way from attaching the same importance to elder abuse as we are to child abuse and in significant ways, the abuse is more complex, given the different legal status of older people and the often lengthy history of unsatisfactory family relationships (Decalmer and Glendenning, 1993; Rowlings, 1995). However, as Department of Health Guidance recognises (DH, 2000) both health care and social services staff need to develop skills in the identification and assessments of elder abuse and in the methods of treatment and intervention that can reduce the risk of recurrence. This is no less necessary in the management and inspection of residential centres and nursing homes, where mental and/or physical frailty increase vulnerability to abusive practice.

So far, this section has identified mostly practice issues. Nevertheless, there is one organisational issue that is of particular relevance and will continue to be dominant over the next few years. This is the relationship between health and social services. One of the aims of the community care reforms was to see greater collaboration between these two services in the provision of community care. Some would say that what happened was an unequal partnership in which hospitals have reduced their provision for older people and social services have to deal with the consequences of a reduction in the number of beds for older people, quicker discharges of elderly patients back to their own homes when they still had some need of care, and insufficient specialist resources, especially for older people with mental health problems (Lewis and Glennerster, 1996). The health service and social services are the two major purchasers of care for older people and for many receiving community care, social and medical needs will be closely associated and will require input from both services. It is in recognition of the importance of the health-social care interface that governments have instituted policies to drive collaborative working at both the strategic level (e.g. through joint purchasing) and the practice level (e.g. through shared assessment). The National Service Framework for the Care of Older People (in England) and the Joint Future Policy Initiative (in Scotland) are evidence of the political determination to achieve integrated health and social care services at all levels.

This chapter began with a discussion of the broader issues and it is to these that we have now returned through this reference to relationships between health and social services. Like so many aspects of community care for older people, there is much uncertainty about how things will develop and how fast they will do so. What is very clear, though, is that improvement and progress must be multi-dimensional. It is not just a question of more money if we do not know how best to spend it. We may need more resources but we may also need different ones or less of some and more of others. And professional practice must continue to improve so that older people and their informal carers can access higher levels of knowledge and expertise. Achieving progress in the context of such uncertainty is the challenge that lies ahead.

Chapter 4

Probation Work With Victims of Crime

Brian Williams

The probation service in England and Wales has been involved in offering support to the victims of crime for more than twenty years, but this area of work is little known. This chapter will explore the nature of probation involvement with victims, and some possible reasons for the low profile of such work. In recent years, there has been intense political controversy in North America and in Europe about the needs and rights of victims. This has inevitably affected the nature of the services provided to them, and the consequences for probation work with victims will be examined.

The Probation System

The probation service in England and Wales is now organised on a national basis, although local probation areas retain some discretion about exactly how services are delivered. In Scotland and Northern Ireland, different systems operate. To avoid undue complication, these separate arrangements are not discussed in what follows (but see Hamai et al., 1995 on the Scottish system). The probation service in England and Wales has increasingly been subject to central government control over funding and priorities since the early 1980s, culminating in the creation of the National Probation Service in 2001.

The primary responsibility of the probation service in England and Wales is to provide services to the courts. The main duties are:

- The provision of advice and information about offenders to the courts, in order to assist in sentencing decisions (primarily by providing written Pre-Sentence Reports [PSRs] and Specific Sentence Reports [SSRs] on defendants prior to sentence and information about defendants applying for bail; see Dominey, 2002).
- The implementation of community sentences, by designing, providing and promoting effective programmes for the supervision of offenders in the community (including for example community service schemes (now known

officially as Community Punishment Orders) individual supervision under probation orders – now re-named Community Rehabilitation Orders).
- Helping prisoners, before and after their release, to lead law-abiding lives.
- Crime prevention (from 1984), and the reduction of the effects of crime upon victims (from 1990) including a statutory duty (since 2001) to maintain contact with victims of crime in more serious cases who wish to be kept informed of the progress of the offender (see Tudor, 2002).
- And (from 1992) to work in partnership with other agencies in pursuit of these duties (Home Office, 1994).
- Also (since 2000) the probation service has been required to contribute staff to multi-agency Youth Offending Teams working with people under eighteen and their victims (Williams, 2000).

The last three sets of responsibilities were added fairly recently, and in some ways they sit uneasily with the other roles. The crime prevention duty is the least well defined of all (see Sampson and Smith, 1992; Sanders and Senior, 1994). The introduction of responsibilities for crime prevention, work with victims and the duty to work in partnership with other agencies has further reduced the offender focus of the probation service. While there has always been competition within probation services for the resources necessary to fulfil the various roles of the agency, this has intensified in the period since 1984: it was then that the government first intervened to require the service to make decisions about its priorities (Home Office, 1984; Lloyd, 1986). Since then, the degree of central government direction has increased and the internal competition for staff and funding to undertake particular aspects of the work of the service has gathered pace correspondingly.

Work with Victims of Crime

Probation officers have always had informal contact with some victims of crime: for example, when working with perpetrators of spousal assault or sexual abuse of children belonging to the same family as the offender. This contact with victims is a salutary reminder of the consequences of crime, and victim perspectives necessarily shape and inform workers' responses to offenders. Victims' organisations have, however, frequently complained that criminal justice agency personnel, including probation staff, show insufficient understanding of victims' needs and feelings (Chelimsky, 1981; Home Office, 1990; Zedner, 2002; Victim Support, 1995; Kosh and Williams, 1995; HMIP, 2003).

Victim support schemes and probation

From its foundation in 1974, the National Association of Victim Support Schemes (now known simply as 'Victim Support') has required its local schemes to include a probation officer or a social worker in the membership of their management committees. In practice, there is invariably a probation representative. During that time, Victim Support has grown from one local project to a national network of nearly 400 covering the whole of the UK. Although this has presented the probation service with some resourcing problems at times, it has maintained at least a formal presence on schemes' management committees. In most areas, the probation contribution has been considerably greater. Probation staff, often senior ones, have not only been involved in management committee activities but also in volunteer training, staff supervision, fundraising and other work. Many local schemes were started at the initiative of probation officers.

Government policy towards victims has taken a number of different directions during the two decades since Victim Support began (see below), and this has inevitably affected the degree of priority given by the probation service to this aspect of its work. With the publication of the Victim's Charter in 1990, it was clear that extra resources would have to be dedicated to probation work with victims – and if necessary, diverted from other areas of probation practice. Before 1990, the picture was very much more confusing, and probation staff tended to be encouraged to give time to local Victim Support schemes without receiving much credit for this activity. Back in the 1970s, they had been actively discouraged from expending probation resources upon links with Victim Support (Holton and Raynor, 1988). Inevitably, therefore, the degree of enthusiasm and commitment displayed by probation officers varied considerably from one scheme to another. In some, probation staff were the founders and the main link with statutory agencies, while in others they were more like 'sleeping partners'.

The increased emphasis on victim work in the 1990s coincided with a period of severe financial restrictions on the public sector: until the late 1980s, the probation service had continued to experience modest annual increases in its budget. By the early 1990s, it was clear that cash limits on expenditure were to be introduced (Beaumont, 1995), and although these were initially fairly lenient, they resulted in staff redundancies by 1994. In the context of an expanding workload, this meant that innovation in the field of victim support was relatively slow, gaining pace again only after 2000 when resource constraints eased. With the introduction of a statutory requirement to work with victims in 2001, additional resources were made available specifically for this purpose, but this coincided with staff shortages.

In terms of probation services' relationships with Victim Support schemes, these continued to vary considerably even within individual probation areas (see for example the study of one county carried out by Kosh and Williams, 1995). Everything depended upon the degree of commitment to the work displayed by individuals, teams and service management at local level. The initial version of the Victim's Charter had no statutory force (Mawby and Walklate, 1994), and in practice it was implemented only partially and gradually (Tudor, 2002). Victim Support schemes themselves had some difficulty during this period in areas where the number of referrals was increasing more quickly than suitable volunteers could be recruited and trained to work with them (Russell, 1990).

The provisions of the Victim's Charter

The provisions of the first Victim's Charter, as far as probation was concerned, included:

- *Making contact, wherever possible, with victims or victims' families in cases where life sentence prisoners are being considered for release to check whether they:*
  ...have anxieties about the offender's release (particularly when it may be appropriate to meet these anxieties by imposing restrictions on where the offender lives, works or goes). (Home Office, 1990: 21)
- *Encouragement to consider three questions: Firstly, how far does the service work with the victims and their representative groups? Secondly, what consideration is given to victims' interests in aspects of the probation service's work? Thirdly are release plans for life sentence prisoners from prison prepared with due regard to the victim's (or the victim's family's) wishes and interests?*

The references to victims' families reflect the fact that most prisoners serving life sentences have committed murder or manslaughter, although the life sentence is increasingly being used for other offences such as rape.

Subsequently, the Home Office began to increase its direct influence over probation practice by issuing a series of detailed guidelines regulating work with clients and other agencies (Bailey, 1995). These National Standards included an elaboration of the Victim's Charter provisions relating to consultation with victims before the release of lifers, and extended these to cover other offenders being considered for release on parole (Home Office, 1992; Home Office, 1995). They require probation officers to:

...arrange for the victim or victim's family to be contacted within two months of sentence and offered the opportunity of being kept informed of the sentence (and, in due course, of expressing any concerns...when...release [is] being considered.

(Home Office, 1995: 45)

This recognises that there were difficulties in implementing the Victim's Charter provisions retrospectively: some victims were contacted unexpectedly, many years after the offence, and found this traumatic and unhelpful (Kosh and Williams, 1995). The new arrangements should ensure that the victims remain in control of the process: they are free to decline to keep in contact, and to cut off such contact with the probation service at a later stage if they wish.

Further contact with victims or their families is required in cases where they have indicated their wish to be kept in touch with the prisoner's progress. Particularly important changes relate to the following:

- Probation officers ascertaining victims' concerns before writing reports about offenders who are released under the 'automatic conditional release' arrangements (i.e. those serving shorter sentences), or about prisoners who are being considered for parole (i.e. those sentenced to four years or over).
- Consultation with Social Services Departments about arrangements for the supervision of offenders who have been convicted of offences against children.
- Additional conditions governing the terms of release of offenders where victims have expressed particular concerns (Home Office, 1995).

These changes have had profound implications for the work of the probation service, and they have occurred at a time when victims of crime have been a matter of constant political controversy. These issues will be considered further in the next section. Other developments in probation practice occurred during the 1980s without government pressure. There was an increasing tendency to try in one way or another to incorporate victims' perspectives in individual and group work with offenders under probation supervision. There also seems to have been a change in the culture of the probation service since the late 1970s when its staff saw themselves as almost exclusively concerned with offenders: increasingly, staff became involved in supporting individual victims they came across in the course of their work. This arose from a recognition that 'the system was too offender-orientated' (Mawby and Gill, 1987: 187).

A revised Victim's Charter was published in 1996, changing the criteria for victim contact work. This meant that probation had a responsibility to offer victims information and to collect information from the about the impact of the offence, in all cases where the offender was sentenced to four years' imprisonment or more. In 2001, this was further extended to cover all offenders imprisoned for one year or more, which brought this work much closer to the mainstream of probation work because of the sheer numbers involved (Tudor, 2002).

Probation group work and victim perspectives

Both in prisons and in the community, probation officers work with offenders in groups. Some of this work arises from the need to impart particular types of information to large numbers of people; the use of group work is then dictated largely by resources (for example, pre-release groups for prisoners). In other cases, group work is used because group dynamics can be a powerful way of involving clients in thinking about changing their behaviour, the obvious examples being offending behaviour groups and group work with sex offenders. In all these different types of groups, victim awareness work has sometimes been incorporated.

Other prison-based groupwork has depended more centrally upon probation involvement, although other 'civilian' prison staff such as chaplains, psychologists and teachers may be involved. Thus, convicted burglars were brought into contact with victims of burglary in a prison-based scheme called Victims and Offenders in Conciliation (VOIC). This was intended both to influence the future behaviour of the offenders and to help victims come to terms with being burgled. The victims directly challenged the offenders' rationalisations for their burglaries, and also found out about burglars' motivation. They were accompanied by Victim Support staff or police for the first session, and the other group staff prevented undue conflict at the remaining sessions. There is some evidence that both victims and offenders derived benefit from the project (Launay and Murray, 1989). Thus, offending behaviour was addressed with the help of victims and in such a way that it was helpful to them too. Increasingly, however, such local initiatives have been replaced by nationally-accredited programmes with a victim awareness component.

There has been a considerable growth in prison group work with sexual offenders, and this has been accompanied by an expansion of attempts to increase offenders' empathy for victims. In one American project, victims have been trained to work with mentally disordered sex offenders on their attitudes to women and to the victims of their offences (Annis, Mathers and Baker, 1984). Most British probation workers would regard this as too risky an experiment, although the Florida project appeared to work successfully, changing dangerous offenders' attitudes without jeopardising the victims' recovery. In England and Wales, the incorporation of an element of victim awareness into the national Sex Offender Treatment Programme has been the favoured approach.

This national programme was widely criticised when it was first introduced, because it was staffed by workers who had received very different levels of professional training. The prison officers in particular had little preparation for the intense and challenging experience of working with groups of sexual offenders who were encouraged to disclose details of their illegal activities in what was meant to be a safe and therapeutic environment. The resources allocated to the groups were inadequate and there was no agreement about the values underlying the programme (Sampson, 1994). The programme was nevertheless imposed centrally, replacing existing provision, which in places was quite sophisticated and well developed, with a national curriculum. Improvements have since been made, and the programme is being thoroughly evaluated, with a national system of accreditation.

The scarce resource of therapeutic regimes at Grendon Underwood prison should also be mentioned at this point, although the units are run by psychiatrists with probation officers, psychologists and prison officers in subordinate roles. This was the only 'psychiatric' prison in England and Wales until recently, although another has recently opened and the prison service plans to open more when resources permit. Serious offenders, many of them murderers and rapists, are moved to Grendon at their own request for extremely intensive therapy in a therapeutically and personally safe environment, which has survived largely outside the prevalent prison subculture of violent masculine competition. Its success rate is encouraging given the intractable nature of the problems and attitudes its inmates bring; many have served several long prison sentences before getting the opportunity to attend (Genders and Player, 1995; Taylor, 2000).

Probation and Youth Offending Team work with individual victims of crime

With the introduction of the Youth Offending Teams (YOTs), some specialist probation staff have joined the new teams on secondment. They are responsible, with their colleagues from other agencies, for supervising young offenders on Reparation Orders and a range of other such activities, and may also work with the police officers seconded to the teams in direct contact with the victims of young offenders (Williams, 2000). Since the introduction of Referral Orders under 1999 legislation introduced nationally in 2001, all young offenders appearing before the Youth Court for the first time (except in very minor and very serious cases) are passed on to meetings of a Panel which includes one YOT and two community representatives. The Panels construct what amounts to a treatment plan in consultation with the young person and (if they choose to become involved) the victim. There is a presumption in favour of including an element of reparation, direct or indirect, in all such plans.

Problems in Practice

The changes discussed above have been quite difficult to achieve, and the probation service has responded slowly to many of the new initiatives for reasons already mentioned. Some changes have been made without much consultation, at a time when probation officers in England and Wales feel that their professionalism and autonomy are under attack. Others have every appearance of being made for political reasons, and many both in and outside the probation service regret the trend towards politicising victim issues. Pressures on funding, and the additional pressure created by a large number of other central government initiatives, which necessitate radical and rapid change in other areas of the probation service's work, have also hampered developments. In these sections, a few examples of such problems relating directly to probation practice will be briefly given.

Victim Support schemes and probation

The difficulties experienced by probation staff wishing to participate in and encourage the development of Victim Support schemes have already been referred to above.

Relations between the Service and Victim Support vary from scheme to scheme and area to area. With the publication of the Victim's Charter, which came as a complete surprise to most probation staff, the urgent necessity of discussions between Victim Support and probation at local level became obvious. Government policy on relationships between the probation service and voluntary agencies has at times been dominated by economic considerations, to an extent, which confuses matters when the two are prepared to co-operate on a friendly basis without any money changing hands (Kosh and Williams, 1995; Humphrey, Pease and Carter, 1993).

The political rhetoric about victims of crime grew louder in the late 1980s, and the probation service may have realigned itself in terms of Victim Support during that time. What it did not do, to any significant extent, was to set up financial partnerships. Probation staff continued, in rather a patchy and *ad hoc* way, to give their time and general support to local schemes and to refer individual clients. In some areas, experimental probation projects involved Victim Support schemes without establishing formal partnerships for the purpose (Launay and Murray, 1989; Trotter, 1990; Porter, 1990; Nation, 1993).

The changing policies of central government were reflected in some confusion on the part of probation workers at local level. Work with community agencies had been actively discouraged in the 1970s, then in 1983, the Home Office began quoting Victim Support as 'a model of how probation officers could work to promote community involvement in criminal justice problems' (Holtom and Raynor, 1988: 22), although there was no sign of additional resources being provided on any scale to facilitate this work. In the early 1990s, when funding cuts began to seem likely, work with Victim Support was seen by some probation services as dispensable, not a core priority. As one probation worker put it in 1995, 'It's almost come full circle...we're operating in a different climate...suddenly the Home Office have discovered victims' (Kosh and Williams, 1995: 20). The impression was confirmed with the passage of the 1998 Crime and Disorder Act, which created Reparation Orders and other requirements that Youth Offending Teams engage with the victims of crimes committed by young people – but this aspect of the legislation affects only probation and other staff seconded to specialist posts within the YOTs. More recently, the government and the Youth Justice Board have emphasised the need to make victims more central to the operation of the youth and criminal justice systems, and consultations have taken place on extending the restorative justice initiatives with young offenders to cover adult criminal justice (Home Office, 2003, 2003a) In such an erratic policy climate, it is hardly surprising that the development of local victim projects was an on-off affair.

The Victim's Charter

The Victim's Charter is in many ways a classic example of top-down policy making. Drafted by civil servants with little idea of its implications for probation practice, it was a response to political imperatives. As Mawby and Walklate (1994: 172) have pointed out, 'reading the Victim's Charter as if it were a policy statement reveals its considerable limitations...a political or ideological reading of the document may provide a more fruitful understanding'. This being so, it is perhaps not surprising that probation responses to the Charter were sometimes rather cynical. In its first version, it gave the service one specific new responsibility and invited the service to ask itself three questions, as we have seen above. In this sense, its implications for probation were few and relatively minor. However, on a political level, it implicitly invited the service to realign itself, abandoning its historical priority of providing services for offenders in favour of a more balanced position. Many probation staff welcomed this trend, but the Victim's Charter did little to encourage it in practice.

A new government subsequently announced the introduction of Victim Personal Statements (Clarke, 2000), which should create an opportunity for victims to describe, very early in the case, how the crime has affected them physically, emotionally and financially. These Statements are meant to be seen by all the professionals involved in each case, but in practice the scheme has experienced considerable teething problems and in many areas criminal justice staff never see the reports, although they are collected from victims routinely by the police.

The implementation of the requirement for probation staff to contact victims or their families before prisoners were released proved quite problematic. Prisons needed a large number of reports in a hurry, and victims in some areas were contacted 'out of the blue' long after offences had been committed, causing considerable distress (Kosh and Williams, 1995 gives examples). In other parts of the country, the decision was taken in discussion between probation services and Victim Support schemes not to implement the new provision retrospectively, anticipating the danger of causing problems of this kind. In yet other areas, sophisticated arrangements were made to implement the Charter commitment (Williams, 1999). Not surprisingly, victims' organisations were disgruntled about the wide range of responses to the Victim's Charter, which initially had no statutory force. The government responded by laying down detailed guidelines in National Standards. When the Inspectorate came to examine probation work with victims of crime, it found a mixed picture in which there was much good practice but also a lack of central, policy direction and considerable variations between the quality of work in different areas (HMIP, 2000, 2003). The placing of this work on a statutory basis from 2001 encouraged greater consistency, and the National Probation service issued detailed guidelines about how it should be done.

Experiments in victim/offender mediation

Attempts to bring individual offenders and 'their' victims together in order to create opportunities for the offenders to apologise and/or repair some of the damage, illustrate the policy confusion about probation work with victims.

Probation staff, as in the case of other work involving victims, were anxious to avoid compromising themselves in the eyes of either victims or offenders. Ways were found of achieving this, although probation officers at first seemed largely to retain the primary allegiance to offenders, which their training and experience encouraged (Davis, 1992). The criminal justice system is enormously powerful, and defendants' rights undoubtedly need protecting. There seemed to be a danger that they might be jeopardised by the hasty introduction of mediation and reparation projects, and probation staff went to great pains to avoid this (Galaway, 1985). Experimental projects came and went in the late 1980s, and the policy agenda changed (Tudor, 2002). The staff that had spent considerable time and energy overcoming the problems thrown up by attempting mediation were left high and dry, and there was a suspicion that policy was being driven by politics rather than by the interests of victims (Mawby and Walklate, 1994; Elias, 1994). Genuinely creative efforts to change the orientation of the criminal justice system, and to move it away from a concern with the formal processing of offenders at the expense of the interests of victims, were mislaid in the process. The 1998 Crime and Disorder Act institutionalised reparation with the victims of young offenders, but tacked this restorative approach onto the existing retributive system, reducing the likelihood of substantial changes in the court's approach towards victims (Williams, 2000). This was remedied to some extent with the introduction of referral orders soon afterwards, but the restorative system remained an add-on to a largely (and increasingly) punitive system.

Interestingly, these concerns are now resurfacing in other countries and in different ways. The notion of restorative justice, derived in part from traditional methods of doing justice among Aboriginal peoples in Canada and New Zealand, is arousing considerable interest there and elsewhere (see for example Consedine, 1995; Hamai et al., 1995). Only if the whole issue of criminal victimisation can be depoliticised will these initiatives stand any real chance of success.

The Political Agenda

The government and the main opposition party in the United Kingdom share a concern to appear 'tough on crime'. This has been translated into specific changes affecting the criminal justice system, but as we have seen, the resources needed for any real alteration to the basis of the system have not always been made available.

There is a need for more rigorous thinking about who victims of crime actually are. The Association of Chief Officers of Probation commissioned research, which shows that there is an enormous overlap between offenders and victims: criminal victimisation is most common in certain poorer areas, and it is in these areas that offenders tend to live. They are themselves frequently the victims of crime (Peelo *et al.*, 1992; Boswell, 1996). Probation practitioners involved with victims have taken on board this complexity (Kosh and Williams, 1995), as have probation managers, but not the political decision-makers.

Indeed, recent criminal justice policy in the UK (and indeed in North America) has been only very selectively informed by research. Glib, superficial, 'commonsense' pronouncements make better television sound-bites. It seems to me very important that the probation service should use its knowledge and experience of work with victims of crime to raise the public and political debate about their treatment above this level wherever possible. There is an obvious problem with this: the probation service is likely to defend its core territory when it feels under threat, and at present, it is threatened as never before. Professional discretion is reduced by a series of increasingly prescriptive National Standards and directives from the National Probation Service; the probation service is criticised by politicians, often apparently unfairly. As Woodhouse and Pengelly (1991: 27) presciently put it, 'It is hard to think about collaboration when you are defending the last ditch of your own professional identity'.

Meanwhile, issues concerning victims of crime have become increasingly politicised, and Victim Support has been forced to compete with the probation service (and with other, more explicitly politically motivated, voluntary organisations such as Rape Crisis Centres) for funding. There is a natural tendency for all these organisations to defend their own interests, and for the strongest to prevail. Victims of crime have no single criminal justice agency to protect their interests (Shapland, 1988). Recent political initiatives to involve victims in the criminal justice system seem to have been motivated more by the desire to legitimate strengthening the social control of offenders than to make any real improvement in the position of the victims. Indeed, the political rhetoric marginalises and weakens the victim's position by portraying them as helpless and 'innocent' (Walklate, 1989) rather than as ordinary people who have suffered a particular type of remediable misfortune.

Chapter 5

Supporting Disabled People

Kirsten Stalker and Cathy Spencer

Introduction

Disabled people have got so much to offer. It would be better if people stopped looking at everything we can't do and looked at what we can do.

(Peter Flynn, 1998: 27)

The need for a change in attitudes towards disabled people is highlighted as 'the way forward' by Peter Flynn, who himself has a learning disability. This chapter will argue that, while social workers cannot single-handedly change society and its attitudes towards disabled people, they *can* be involved in promoting and supporting disabled people's rights and aspirations – to independence, self-determination and inclusion. As Oliver and Sapey (1999: 32) comment, 'In working with disabled people the social work task is...one of...helping them to locate the personal, social, economic and community resources to enable them to live life to the full'.

This chapter will explore the social work task in relation to disabled people, taking account of underlying theoretical perspectives and relevant social policy and legislation. The latter includes the NHS and Community Care Act 1990, the Disability Discrimination Act 1995 and the Human Rights Act 1999, as well as more recent developments such as the reviews of services to people with learning disabilities north and south of the border (Scottish Executive 2000, Department of Health 2001) and the Supporting People Programme (2001). Some of the tensions and constraints underlying social work theory and practice in this field will be explored. Lastly, the discussion will focus on more innovative ways of working – such as direct payments, person-centred planning and user involvement, along with future directions for social work training and practice.

Background

According to the 'Labour Force Survey' (Winter 1999/2000), there are over 6.4 million disabled people of working age in Great Britain, accounting for nearly a fifth of the working age population (Disability Rights Commission, 2000). These statistics are based on a broad, medical definition of disability as a long-term (and/or progressive) condition 'which has a substantial adverse impact on (a person's) day-to-day activities or limits the kind or amount of work' they are able to perform (Disability Rights Commission, 2000). The survey therefore includes people over the age of sixteen and under retirement age who have a physical impairment, sensory impairment, learning disability or mental ill-health, (increasingly referred to by service users/survivors as 'mental distress'), and encompasses people with a wide range and degree of impairment. This chapter is about social work with all these people, except those with mental distress, for whom some of the issues and much of the policy and practice differ, and who are the subject of chapter six. In addition, it should be noted that the majority of people with impairments are actually above state pension age, and therefore were not included in the Labour Force Survey. Older people are discussed in chapter three, although many of the issues explored here may be equally relevant in relation to older disabled people.

In terms of learning disability, definitions and terminology remain a contested area. For example, in the authors' experience, many individuals prefer the term 'people with learning *difficulties*'. This debate continues that which surrounded the move from the use of such terms as 'mental handicap' or 'mental deficiency', which were seen as stigmatising and negative (Thompson, 1998). The debate is reflected in government publications with, for example, 'Supporting People' (2001) referring to 'learning difficulties' whereas the White Paper 'Valuing People' (2001) refers to 'learning disabilities'. The latter term is used here, with some personal reservations, because it is the 'official' term endorsed by the Department of Health and the Scottish Executive. The category refers to a very wide range of people, but all of them have in common a life-long condition that affects their ability to learn. Although the cause of the learning disability is often unknown, it may be identified as a genetic condition (the most well known of which is Down's syndrome), or as due to brain damage caused before or during birth. In many cases, environmental factors contribute towards learning disability, and often the cause may be described as 'multi-factorial' (involving a number of different factors).

While statistics vary according to different surveys, it is estimated by organisations working in the field of learning disability (for example MENCAP and the British Institute of Learning Disabilities), that 1.2 million people in the UK have a learning disability, making this the single most common form of impairment. Of these, approximately 200,000 will be classed as having a 'severe learning disability'. People who have a learning disability may have additional sensory and/or physical impairments, speech and communication impairments and/or epilepsy, and some may behave in ways that challenge those who provide support. They are also more likely than the general population to experience mental health difficulties.

In the past, many disabled people – and particularly those with multiple impairments and/or learning disabilities – lived in large hospitals or institutions, segregated from the rest of the community. Residents led monotonous, bleak and deprived lives, subject to mass regimentation. Sometimes people with physical impairments also found themselves in such institutions, usually because there was nowhere else for them to go. However, it was not until the 1960s that political and public dissatisfaction with long-stay institutions erupted, fuelled by a series of scandals about poor physical conditions and alarming incidents of misconduct by staff. In spite of such impetus, it has taken some considerable time to achieve reform. As recently as 1971, when the organisation CMH (the Campaign for the Mentally Handicapped – now renamed VIA, Values into Action) was established, it estimated that 65,000 people were living in long-stay 'mental handicap hospitals'. Even at the end of the twentieth century, according to VIA's campaigning material, there were still approximately 10,000 people in 'long-stay' institutions or hospitals. However, this type of environment is now widely held to be unacceptable, and recent government reviews of services to people with learning disabilities stated that the remaining hospitals were to close by 2004 in England and Wales (Department of Health, 2001) and 2005 in Scotland (Scottish Executive, 2000). Today, disabled people live in a variety of settings – some with their partners and families, some with small groups of other people, others in supported lodgings, or in their own homes. In Scotland, for example, 23 per cent of people with learning disabilities known to local authorities have their own tenancies (Scottish Executive, 2004a).

Significantly, for services providing social and health care, the number of disabled people is rising steadily because of progress in medical science and social developments. Improved neo-natal and post-natal care has led to the survival of children born with multiple impairments and complex needs. Moreover, the life expectancy of many disabled people has improved significantly in recent years due to advances in medical and social care. For example, research by Janicki et al. (1999), suggests that fifty per cent of all people with learning disabilities now have the same life expectancy as the general population (cited in Thompson, A., 1999). This situation is very different from that of a generation ago, when it was common for parents of a child born with significant impairment to be told by doctors to expect the child to die at a relatively young age. Such developments, while undeniably positive, have shown up deficiencies in support services. As Thompson, D. (1993) argues, additional resources must be provided in order to ensure that the needs of the growing population of older disabled people are adequately met.

The Present-day Experiences of Disabled People

A comprehensive picture of the impact of being disabled in the United Kingdom today has been provided by a series of reports. These have looked at both the experiences of disabled people themselves and public attitudes towards disability. A study conducted for SCOPE in 1994 by Lamb and Layzell, which involved consultation through postal questionnaires with 1,500 disabled people, revealed depressing results. The research summary cites 'the isolation, anger and frustration that disabled people feel when confronted by thoughtlessness, prejudice and inadequate services'. One in three respondents had been refused a service or turned away from a public place; nearly half felt that people did not really listen to what they said they needed or made incorrect assumptions about this, and over half of those expressing an opinion reported they had been refused a job interview or a job itself because of their impairment. The latter finding is supported by data from the Disability Rights Commission survey (DRC 2000), which revealed that disabled people are about seven times as likely as non-disabled people to be out of work and claiming benefits.

A report commissioned by the Leonard Cheshire Foundation, a voluntary organisation (Knight and Brent, 1998), also highlighted the social exclusion and discrimination experienced by disabled people. In particular, the report suggested that this has its roots in the attitudes of the general population. It found that 53 per cent of the public have no regular contact with disabled people, an alarmingly high percentage given the proportion of disabled people within the population. Nearly a quarter of those surveyed admitted to feeling 'self-conscious' and 'awkward' in the presence of a disabled person. Although there were some more optimistic findings, the overall picture is of intractable and detrimental perceptions of disability amongst non-disabled people. As John Knight, Leonard Cheshire's director of social policy puts it, 'There has been no significant movement in the attitudes of non-disabled people towards disability, and disabled people are still associated with charity, doctors and sympathy' (cited in Winchester, 2000).

Worse still are the common experiences of disabled people from black and minority ethnic communities. Research has revealed the double burden of discrimination and disadvantage faced by black and Asian disabled people (Council of Disabled People, 2000; Jeewa, 1998). Moreover, not only do they experience both racism and disablist attitudes and treatment on a daily basis, but also they are 'doubly invisible' to the services and support they need. Many feel excluded from local service provision that continues to be largely euro-centric in nature; at the same time, they may also feel their needs are ignored by their own community groups.

Finally, in this section, we should not forget that the lives of some disabled people are blighted by abuse. The fact that disabled people are particularly vulnerable to abuse, and indeed that abuse has been occurring systematically in certain 'care' homes and other environments, has only recently been recognised. Disabled people are more likely to experience abuse (physical, sexual, emotional, financial and/or institutional) than the rest of the population for various reasons. These include the fact that any communication difficulties may make it hard for them to complain or be understood; the way in which the historical context of attitudes towards and treatment of disabled people almost 'condones' abuse; the possible need for care of an intimate nature; and enforced dependency on others which can lead to a sense of disempowerment and lack of self-esteem. Procedures for protecting 'vulnerable adults' (including disabled people), and following up on suspicions or allegations of abuse, have now been developed by most local authorities. However, these are a long way behind the introduction of child protection procedures, and do not have the statutory weight that is afforded to child protection work through the Children Act 1989 and the Children (Scotland) Act 1995. All too often, in one author's experience, perpetrators of the abuse of disabled people are not brought to trial or find themselves exonerated of any crime, because of the intransigence of the criminal justice system and the prejudiced attitudes of many of those who work within the system (see also, McCarthy 1999).

Theoretical Perspectives

Since the latter part of the twentieth century, two main philosophies have been influential in the development of services for disabled people, and the concepts underlying them are highly relevant to social work practice today. The ethos of *normalisation* has had its chief impact in the area of learning disabilities, while the *social model of disability* has been most influential in relation to people with physical and/or sensory impairment. There are broad similarities between the two theories, in that they would both support a 'collective' or inclusive view of disability, but there are also some significant differences.

Normalisation

The term 'normalisation' has lost some credibility in recent years, but the ideas and values which underlie it – revolutionary at the time the theory was introduced – are still important today. Normalisation originated in Scandinavia, and was pioneered by Nirje (1969) and Bank-Mikkelson (1980). Its central theme at that time was that services should be developed in such a way as to enable people with learning disabilities to enjoy 'patterns of life and conditions of everyday living which are as close as possible to the regular circumstances and ways of life of society' (Nirje, 1980: 33).

Thus, for example, disabled people have the right to experience the same sort of daily and weekly routines, age-appropriate activities, relationships, economic standards and level of self-determination as the rest of the population. At this early stage in its development, 'normalisation' amounted to a series of principles which were intended to shape service delivery, but which did not add up to a coherent theoretical framework (Emerson, 1992). However, the idea was taken up and radicalised by Wolf Wolfensberger in the United States (1972, 1980).

Wolfensberger highlighted the phenomenon of *labelling*, through which negative assumptions and low expectations are attached to people with learning disabilities, leading to a 'self-fulfilling prophecy' where few opportunities are offered to develop potential, and the stereotyped beliefs of others are reinforced. He showed how people with learning disabilities are systematically devalued in society and he analysed the way this process is perpetuated through the use of social imagery, for example, through the denigrating images ascribed to them in literature and the media. Smith and Brown (1992) emphasise the importance of Wolfensberger's analysis in moving beyond the 'how' and 'why' of devaluation towards searching for ways of challenging and overcoming it. Indeed, there can be no doubt that normalisation has had a major positive impact on the nature and quality of service provision. By helping to raise awareness of the bleak lives led by many people in segregated institutions, and of the subsequent damaging emotional and psychological effects, the ethos of normalisation was an important influence on the development of community care policies.

Nevertheless, there are serious criticisms to be made of some of its underlying implications. Wolfensberger's original formulation of normalisation contends that, in order to promote their integration in, and acceptance by, the community at large, people with learning disabilities should attempt to 'blend in' by being as 'ordinary', conventional and unobtrusive as possible. This emphasis on conformity leaves little room for variation and diversity, either at the level of individual taste or preference, or at a socio-cultural level, be it in terms of race, gender, sexual orientation or, indeed, any other significant dimension. In this sense, normalisation can, ironically, be seen as itself devaluing disabled people; its insistence on the importance of associating with non-disabled people, for example, seems to imply that it is undesirable for people with learning disabilities to associate with each other. It has also been pointed out that, by exhorting people with learning disabilities to adopt the views and values of the status quo, normalisation expects them to take on the perspective of the very people who are devaluing them (Smith and Brown, 1992). Thus, it can be seen as an inherently conservative philosophy, failing to challenge the attitudinal and structural factors which account for many of the barriers faced by people with learning disabilities. As Brown and Walmsley argue:

> ...instead of remedying devaluation by promoting 'normal' social roles and images, a more appropriate strategy for change may be for oppressed groups to re-assess themselves, disown the negative projections put upon them by others and demand that the world changes to accommodate them.
>
> (Brown and Walmsley, 1997: 232)

Much of Wolfensberger's work – both in relation to his original principle of normalisation, and his development of the theory into 'Social Role Valorisation' – is written in a dense theoretical style, which lessens its accessibility. In contrast, the work of his former colleague John O'Brien is presented in a relatively simple and straightforward manner. Furthermore, O'Brien re-stated the importance of individual choice and control. He has written extensively on advocacy and social inclusion, but is best known for setting out the 'Five Service Accomplishments' (1987), targets towards which community services should aim if they are to realise the principles of normalisation. The accomplishments are: community presence; choice; respect; competence (opportunities for people to reach their full potential by developing a range of skills) and participation. O'Brien's work has had a significant impact on provision for people with learning disabilities in the UK, with many services identifying the 'five accomplishments' as their main value base (see for example Walker, 1995; Riddell et al., 1997).

The social model of disability

The social model of disability derives from the experiences of disabled people who argue that disability is not an inevitable result of impairment, but of a society organised for the benefit and convenience of non-disabled people (Oliver, 1990). Professional policy and practice within social work and other 'caring professions' have for many years been dominated by the medical model of disability. As its name implies, this model equates disability with chronic illness, ascribes a 'sick' role to the individual and focuses on physical 'dysfunction'. People are classified according to their particular diagnosis or *impairment*. From this perspective, the appropriate professional response is aimed at improving the individual's physical or functional capacities, the limitations or perceived inadequacies of which are seen as the sole cause of any difficulties. The medical model is linked to broader psychodynamic theories which dominated social work training and practice in the past, but which have less influence today. The experience of being or becoming disabled is assumed to constitute a continuing personal tragedy, triggering a grief reaction in the same way that bereavement would do. It is up to the individual to adapt both to the tragedy and to society (Oliver, 1990). Certain individuals may be judged to have had outstanding success in overcoming the odds against them, thus attaining the status of 'hero'. More often, however, disabled people are thought to be in constant mourning for their lost or missing 'wholeness', and seen as requiring the intervention of 'expert' professionals to attend to their psychological, emotional and practical needs.

In contrast to the medical model, the social model of disability points to the constraints and barriers within society as the source of disability, rather than an individual's actual impairment. Thus, the social model highlights 'the disabling propensities of 'non-disabled' society through its promotion of attitudinal prejudices, physical obstacles and social barriers' (Drake, 1998: 88).

French provides a helpful distinction between 'impairment' and 'disability':

Blindness is impairment but lack of access to written information is a disability – a socially determined state of affairs, which could be solved with more extensive Braille production, more money to pay for readers and the greater use of taped material.

(French, 1992: 17)

The social model is closely associated with the disability movement, a loose contemporary grouping of activists, which campaigns for the reduction or removal of the restrictions imposed upon individuals who have impairments. The disability movement was at the forefront of the campaign for anti-discrimination legislation in Britain that led to the Disability Discrimination Act of 1995, which will be discussed later. The movement has also been highly critical of the numerous voluntary charitable organisations 'for' disabled people which grew up particularly in the first half of the twentieth century and which remain prevalent and influential today. Following a medical model, such organisations often focus on a particular category of impairment and are generally run by non-disabled people. They are seen by many within the disability movement as unrepresentative of those they are aiming to support and as tending towards paternalistic attitudes.

While the social model of disability has been highly influential, certain aspects have been challenged by dissenting voices from within the disability movement itself. It has been criticised for its neglect of gender issues (Morris, 1992, Begum, 1992), while the need to take account of racial issues (Stuart, 1993) and sexual orientation (Corbett, 1995) has also been highlighted. It has been argued that the emphasis on 'disability' within the social model has led to a serious and detrimental underestimation of the significance of impairment. Crow (1996: 66), highlighting the need for a 'fresh look' at the social model, wrote:

> *It is critical that we recognise the ways in which disability and impairment work together. The social model has never suggested that disability represents the total explanation or that impairment doesn't count – that has simply been the impression we have given by keeping our experiences of impairment private and failing to incorporate them into our political analysis.*
>
> (Crow, 1996: 66)

Thomas (1999) has addressed some of these criticisms in her work developing a 'social relational model' of disability. This identifies two types of oppression – one arising from economic and material barriers which affect what disabled people can *do*, the other, which she calls 'psycho-emotional disablism', resulting from social processes and interpersonal behaviour, which affect what disabled people can '*be*' or '*become*'. Here, Thomas is referring to the hostile, hurtful or patronising comments and actions of non-disabled people which those with impairments may face on a daily basis and which can have a profound effect on their self-esteem. In addition, Thomas highlights the significance of 'impairments effects', that is, the implications of living with a particular impairment, which may range from pain, discomfort or fatigue to the inability to perform certain tasks. Not all of these can be 'sorted' by removing physical or social barriers. Thomas' work is important because it embraces the complexity of disability, bringing together the personal and the political dimensions.

Although debate continues about certain aspects of disability theory, the basic concepts of the social model need to be well understood by social workers in order to be incorporated more fully into social work practice. As Oliver and Sapey argue:

> *...social workers need to recognise that disability is a social construction and not necessarily a fixed physical entity, and need to plan their strategies of intervention accordingly.*
>
> (Oliver and Sapey, 1999: 55)

Social Work Practice

As outlined above, the analysis of disability presented in the social model highlights the significance of social, economic and environmental barriers confronting people. It follows that the activities of social workers should be directed at enabling individuals and groups to overcome the disabling effects of such barriers, for example, by helping people seek employment, obtain all the welfare benefits to which they are entitled, and gain access to whatever equipment, adaptations and personal assistance they require to participate fully in mainstream social and economic life (Barnes, 1991). French (1994) argues that social workers should act as a resource to be used by disabled people, rather than providers of care. They have an important role to play in facilitating access to information and material resources, but should carry this out in an enabling rather than a controlling manner. In order to support people in overcoming the disabling effects of disadvantage and discrimination, and to ensure that support is offered in a way that allows people to exercise choice and control, it should be a major priority of social work practice to empower individuals and groups. This is a long, slow process which can take place in a variety of ways: for example, by encouraging self-determination; by creating opportunities for participation in aspects of service provision; through advocacy and by enabling people to become as independent as possible, taking part in mainstream community life rather than being relegated to segregated settings. Each of these activities is discussed in more detail below.

Self-determination

The term 'self-determination' is increasingly used, particularly in the field of learning disability, to refer to important concepts such as choice and control over one's life. Most people would support these ideas in principle. However, putting self-determination into practice presents challenges, particularly in relation to people who have more severe impairments and/or limited communication skills. It is all too easy for social workers and others to make assumptions about an individual's wishes or to presume that s/he does not have the ability to make decisions. In fact, there is a growing body of evidence that, given the right opportunities and support, people who have little or no verbal communication and very high support needs can make choices and achieve self-determination (The Foundation for People with Learning Disabilities, 2000; Bewley, 1999). Bewley argues:

> *Self-determination, in this context…means having the appropriate support to enable you to live life to its full, in the way that suits you. Circles of support have shown how those who may be considered legally unable to consent (because of their learning disability) can be supported to live independently. The individual is at the centre of decision-making and supporters act within a code of practice and statement of commitment, which honours this.*
>
> (VIA newsletter, issue 96)

The important question to be asked, states Bewley, is how *all* disabled people can be supported to achieve self-determination. In exploring this theme, Holman and Bewley (1999) give guidelines as to how someone should act to support an individual's self-determination. These are useful principles for social workers, as well as others more generally described as 'supporters', and include:

- Treating individuals with respect and listening carefully to them.
- Learning about their interests and preferences and helping them to identify the kind of support that will enable them to participate in community life.
- Recognising the social, financial, and personal barriers to the kind of life the individual wants, and assisting them to find ways of overcoming these.
- Understanding the vulnerabilities for their well-being that result from their impairment and personal history, and carefully negotiating safeguards with them that balance risk and safety in a responsible way.
- Encouraging flexibility and creativity with all the resources available so that there is an effective response to their interests, preferences and needs.

Promoting participation

It is now widely accepted that good practice involves promoting user participation in the design, delivery and monitoring of services, and this principle is enshrined in the community care legislation, which will be discussed in the next section.

As part of the 'Living Options in Practice' project, based in London, a continuum of participation by disabled people in service planning was developed, (Fiedler and Twitchin, 1992: 3). This comprised:

- *Information* – Sharing ideas and plans about services and information-giving.
- *Consultation* – Seeking views and advice based on plans, policies and services; ordinary public consultation exercises.
- *Partnership* – Working on an equal basis in setting goals, making plans and deciding funding priorities, including representation on public committees and planning groups.
- *Delegated Control* – Giving authority and money to disabled people to plan and implement services.

The dominant means of participation across Britain is currently consultation. However, as there is no *one* 'user voice', but rather a variety of views and opinions among disabled people, so there should be a range of opportunities for participation, allowing individuals and groups to become involved in the ways that best suit them, depending on choice and circumstance. People with learning disabilities, for example, may find it hard to participate in large formal meetings involving a lot of paperwork and complex discussion of finance and planning. Many will, however, be able to make a positive contribution through informal discussion, provided that good preparation and support are available.

The dissemination of information is crucial to enabling participation at any level. The importance of using different forms of communication is evident, for example, producing information in Braille, in sign language, on video, in large print and in minority ethnic languages.

Promoting real opportunities for participation is time-consuming and can be expensive. A number of strategies can be employed to facilitate the process. Training should be provided both for professionals, and for disabled people, some of whom may lack relevant experience and knowledge. At the same time, it may be helpful to employ, as consultants, other disabled individuals who have specialist knowledge and expertise. Both service users and professionals in one study suggested that a two-tier system of consultation is most useful: one, at a professional formal level; the other, local, informal and very much on users' terms (Stalker and Reddish, 1994). Adequate resources must be made available to enable effective participation, including transport, remuneration of expenses and provision of accessible venues. Efforts should be made to ensure that disabled people from black and minority ethnic communities are included in participatory exercises.

Advocacy

The voices of disabled people are not always heard, let alone listened to. Advocacy – gaining the confidence to speak up for oneself or, alternatively, having someone to speak on one's behalf – is now widely recognised as an important means of enabling people to express their wishes. Simons (1993) identifies four different models of advocacy, as follows:

- *Citizen advocacy:* the development of a supportive, one-to-one relationship between an unpaid private citizen and someone who is vulnerable or at risk of isolation, with the aim of offering some protection to the latter and help to achieve his or her personal goals.
- *Self advocacy:* usually refers to the activities of groups of people with learning disabilities who have come together to voice their collective concerns and campaign for rights. Sometimes such groups are based in a specific service, like a day centre or residential establishment. Other groups are independent of any service; many of these affiliated to the 'People First' movement, which originated in North America and is now a world-wide network with a large number of groups active in the UK.
- *Class advocacy:* involves public support or campaigning for a group or section of people, usually by established voluntary organisations.
- *Professional advocacy:* paid individuals, such as welfare rights workers, advocacy workers, and solicitors, who offer advice and support to anybody who seeks their help.

An overall objective of any form of advocacy should be to empower people. An important aspect of advocacy is to enable individuals to advocate for their own rights wherever possible. Self-advocacy in particular arises out of a recognition that services have traditionally disempowered users. Conflicts of interest can arise if someone advocating on an individual's behalf is, for example: part of the service system; responsible for assessing that person's needs; providing a service or managing budgets. It is therefore important to arrange for an independent advocate wherever possible. Not all individuals will want or need advocacy; in the United Kingdom, advocacy is currently most developed in relation to people with learning disabilities.

Enabling independence and inclusion

In the latter part of the twentieth century, reinforced by the changing theoretical perspectives discussed earlier, significant progress was made in the development of community-based services for disabled people. A working paper entitled 'An Ordinary Life', published by the Kings Fund in 1980, put forward the proposal – quite radical at the time – that disabled people (specifically those with learning disabilities) should be 'in the mainstream of life, living in ordinary houses, in ordinary streets, with the same range of choices as any citizen, and mixing as equals with the other....members of their own community' (cited in Towell, 1990: 115). This vision of social inclusion is still far from being achieved, as seen earlier in our discussion of the present-day experiences of disabled people, and as disabled people themselves testify. The views of members of a self-advocacy group in Bristol, for example, reveal something of what it is like to be a person with a learning disability in the United Kingdom today:

- It...means that lots of other things happen to you – like being sent to day centres, and to live in houses you don't like.
- I did nothing all day (at the day centre). And it's a childish atmosphere...some of the staff treat us like children.
- I have a problem crossing roads, but that doesn't mean that I have to live with lots of other people who can't cross roads. Also, I don't want to be thought of just as a 'bad road crosser'.

(Williams, 1999: 4–5)

Although for many people an 'ordinary life' and social inclusion remain distant aspirations, the fact that principles that promote such aspirations are now widely accepted and discussed has had the positive outcome that, increasingly, disabled people and their families are not prepared to accept the second-rate services of the past. Traditionally, social work services have not prioritised support for disabled people and those services that have been available have been repeatedly criticised for their inflexibility and poor co-ordination. In addition, they have often been provided in large-scale segregated settings. As we have already seen, many disabled people have until fairly recently been accommodated in institutions, and some still live in residential care, often because there is insufficient support available in the community.

The traditional response to the need for daytime occupation has been to provide some form of day centre. Most centres offer a range of small-group activities of a recreational or skills-training nature, and interaction with the wider community is actively encouraged. Authorities that are more progressive are moving away from a 'building-based' service to a more peripatetic model, which includes educational and work opportunities. Without doubt, there is room for far greater use by disabled people of ordinary mainstream leisure and educational facilities. As regards employment, some agencies are involved in supported employment initiatives, whereby disabled people have real jobs, paid at the going rate, in ordinary settings, supported as appropriate by a 'job coach'.

In the area of domiciliary assistance, social services departments have traditionally provided 'home help' services, which offer support with domestic tasks and shopping primarily to older and disabled people. An important aspect of the service, especially for those who are lonely or housebound, is the provision of social contact. In more recent years, authorities have developed more flexible 'home care' services, available in the evenings, early mornings and at weekends. Home carers undertake a wider range of tasks, including, importantly, personal care. 'Support workers' have a more general remit, which relates to enabling disabled people to develop greater independence, for example, by supporting them in independent travel, managing their own money, using mainstream community facilities or attending college. All the above kinds of service are now largely provided by private or voluntary agencies, and purchased by social services through care management, which will be discussed in the next section.

Social Policy and Legislation

Although this chapter is concerned with all disabled people, historically legislation and polices affecting those with physical impairments have, to some extent, been separated from those affecting people with learning disabilities, and subject to different initiatives. In both arenas, however, developments have been greatly influenced by the policy of community care.

This term has been widely used to signify a vast range of health and, primarily, social care arrangements. The following definition, although some years old, remains apt today:

> To the politician, community care is a useful piece of rhetoric; to the sociologist, it is a stick to beat institutional care with; to the civil servant, it is a cheap alternative to institutional care which can be passed to the local authorities for action – or inaction; to the visionary, it is a dream of the new society in which people really do care; to social services departments, it is a nightmare of heightened public expectations and inadequate resources to meet them.
>
> (Jones, Brown and Bradshaw, 1983: 102)

Continuing difficulties in implementing community care polices led to a number of government reports in the 1980s (see for example, Audit Commission, 1986; Griffiths, 1987) which analysed the reasons for slow progress and set out proposals for change. These culminated in the National Health Service and Community Care Act of 1990. This legislation, which applies to all user groups, introduced far-reaching reforms in the structure, funding and organisation of health and social care. Central to the reforms was the statement that 'promoting choice and independence underlies all the Government's proposals' (Secretaries of State for Health and Social Security, 1989, 1.8). Flexible services tailored to meet individual need, offering a range of options and intervening 'no more than is necessary to foster independence', were identified as key components of the new strategy. Disabled people are included among the 'most vulnerable groups' and are therefore entitled to an assessment of their needs, although it was emphasised in the White Paper 'Community Care in the Next Decade and Beyond' (1989) that wherever possible disabled people should take responsibility for their own needs and for managing their own lives.

What then are the main implications of the Community Care Act? This question will be answered firstly from the point of view of social work practice, and secondly in relation to the experiences of disabled people themselves. In respect of social work practice, a key factor was the introduction of the concept of *'care management'*. The role of *care manager* differs in significant respects from that of *social worker*, in particular in having responsibility for allocating and managing resources (including finance). Moreover, it is not necessary to have a social work qualification to be a care manager; among the professional qualifications also regarded as relevant to the role are nursing and occupational therapy. The exact range and nature of the functions carried out by care managers vary somewhat between different local authorities. However, the overall aim of care management is summed up in the Social Services Inspectorate's 'Summary of Practice Guidance' (1991: 7) as 'tailoring services to individual needs'. The seven core tasks that make up the process are described as:

- publishing information
- determining the level of assessment
- assessing need
- care planning
- implementing the care plan
- monitoring
- reviewing.

In theory at least, the emphasis should be on the individual service user as an active partner at the centre of the assessment and care planning process, not just as the passive recipient of 'care' from the professionals. Unfortunately in practice, as Sanderson et al. (1997) suggest, care planning is frequently seen as an office-based administrative process involving excessive paperwork. They argue that the role needs to be seen in a more positive light by practitioners, as the recording of a practical and dynamic series of inter-relationships, between all people involved in the care and support of the individual service user.

Sheppard (1995) argues that community care, and in particular, the concept of care management, 'presents perhaps the greatest challenge to social work for at least twenty years' (cited in McDonald, 1999: 42). It contains, according to Sheppard, elements of both change and continuity. The former involves the 'bureaucratisation of social care' and the inclusion of market principles; while the latter refers to the relevance of core social work approaches such as interpersonal skills, working with social networks and social supports, and task-centred practice. Similarly, Coulshed and Orme (1998) contend that assessment and planning have always been part of social work intervention, and that care management requires the knowledge, values and skills – such as communication, negotiation and mobilising resources – provided by social work education and training.

The role of the care manager arguably offers new challenges for social workers, such as the emphasis on working in partnership with service users and, where appropriate, their family/carers; increased collaboration with other agencies; working within a 'mixed economy of welfare' in which there is much greater involvement from voluntary and private agencies in the provision of care; and looking at more flexible and innovative ways of supporting people in the community. It is increasingly likely that people qualifying as social workers, as well as some with other qualifications, who wish to work with disabled adults in local authority settings will be employed as care managers. Some commentators have argued that this is not a positive development. Oliver and Sapey, for example, contend that:

> *The onset of care management has had the effect of neutralising social work as a radical activity. The development of procedures and regulations for the provision of services along with the limitation of the legitimate role of social work to this instrumental activity has curtailed many of the roles of social workers that were previously undisputed.*
>
> (Oliver and Sapey: 1999: 183)

Some local authorities continue to employ social workers, alongside care managers, to work with disabled people. While there may be some overlap in their functions, this arrangement has definite benefits, in particular in allowing social workers to retain their role of advocating on behalf of service users and, where necessary, challenging assessments of need and decisions made about service provision for an individual, without being directly constrained by tight prioritisation criteria or concerns about financial and resource implications. It is of course crucial, in situations where a service user has both a social worker and a care manager allocated to them, that the two workers liaise and consult with each other.

From the point of view of service users, the community care legislation introduces changes which may appear beneficial in various ways. Among the 'key benefits' of care management identified in the 'Summary of Practice Guidance' (1991: 11–16) are:

- Greater partnership with users and carers.
- Services tailored to individual requirements.
- A commitment to individual care plans.
- Improved opportunities for representation and advocacy.
- A wider choice of services across the statutory and independent sectors.
- A way of meeting more effectively the needs of disadvantaged individuals – including disabled people and those from black and minority ethnic communities.

However, the legislation and associated legislative guidance have been criticised, particularly from within the disability movement, on a number of grounds. Firstly, the emphasis on 'care management' increases professional control over disabled people by requiring the latter to undergo assessment and submit to the 'expertise' of the professional. As Thompson (1993) points out, this assumption that the 'experts' know best about the needs of disabled people retains the influence of the medical model of disability. It is argued in research by Sim, Milner, Love and Lishman (1998) that the NHS and Community Care Act 1990 has failed to reconcile the gap between professionally defined needs (based on functional impairments) and those identified by disabled people themselves. Moreover, Morris (1993: 38) asserts that the aim of 'independent living', seen as central to the NHS and Community Care Act, is actually 'held back by an ideology at the heart of community care policies, which does not recognise the civil rights of disabled people but instead considers them to be dependent people in need of care'.

Secondly, the reforms place great emphasis on the importance of supporting carers, stating, for example, that carers' views must be taken into account wherever possible. It has been argued that, as well as the potential conflict of interest which arises when carers and users have different and sometimes opposing views, the focus on carers maintains disabled people in a state of continuing dependency, rather than promoting real independence. As Oliver and Sapey point out:

> The recognition of carers is itself part of the problem because it reinforces the helper-helped relationship that lies at the heart of the creation of dependency by seeing their needs as relative to the 'burden' caused by the disabled person.
>
> (Oliver and Sapey, 1999: 105)

The policy solution, they argue, lies within the social model analysis:

> ...collective approaches that are based on the inclusion, not the exclusion, of disabled people from mainstream social organisation: in other words the removal of disabling barriers.
>
> (ibid.: 106)

Further criticism has been directed towards the way in which the assessment and care planning process is working in practice within some local authorities. For example, a survey carried out by Frazer and Glick (2000), for the 'Needs Must Coalition', of over 1500 older and disabled people living throughout UK, found that assessments were often subject to lengthy delays and that much of the service provision was of such poor quality that people's welfare and dignity were put at risk. Similarly, a study of two social services departments' assessment procedures and disabled people's access to them (Davis, Ellis and Rummery, 1998) revealed very variable, and often unsatisfactory, practice. For example, most social workers' decisions about access to assessment were influenced by budget considerations; in some assessments the practitioner and the disabled person did not even meet, and disabled people and their carers found assessment encounters with local authority social services departments confusing, fragmentary and often irrelevant to their own concerns and priorities.

It must be hoped that such difficulties in relation to the community care legislation can be remedied, at least to some extent, by two later pieces of legislation. Firstly, the Disability Discrimination Act was passed in 1995 to introduce new measures, which make it unlawful for a disabled person to be discriminated against in the areas of employment, transport, education, access to goods, facilities and services, and the management, buying or renting of land or property. In order to enforce the law, the Disability Rights Commission was established in 2000, and by September of that year, it was receiving an estimated 1,000 calls per week to its helpline (Revans, 2000).

In addition, the Human Rights Act 1998 (which came into force in October 2000), enforces in the UK the rights enshrined within the European Convention on Human Rights. These include the right to 'Freedom from Discrimination' (Article 14) in relation to all the other rights guaranteed under the Convention. Hence, it is unlawful for people to be denied equal access to their rights on the grounds of their 'status', which includes disability. The Human Rights Act touches on many aspects of social care policy and delivery and could be used by disabled people, in principle at least, to challenge sub-standard services as constituting discrimination on the part of local authorities or other agencies.

Finally in this section on social policy and legislation, it is important to mention 'The Same as You?' report, a review of services to people with learning disabilities in Scotland (Scottish Executive, 2000) and the White Paper 'Valuing People: A New Strategy for Learning Disability for the twenty-first Century', the first White Paper on learning disability for thirty years, published by the Department of Health in England 2001. Significantly, these reviews were the first time that people with learning disabilities have been involved in advising the Government on a strategy, through formal Advisory Groups. In England, they produced their own report, *Nothing About Us Without Us* (Department of Health, 2001: 5), which states that '*All services* should include people with learning difficulties properly in everything they do'.

'Valuing People' sets out eleven clear objectives for learning disability services, some relating to outcomes for people, such as good health and fulfilling lives, while others concern systems needed to deliver better outcomes, such as partnership working and workforce training and planning. There are four key principles at the heart of the proposals: legal and civil rights, independence, choice and social inclusion. The intention is to take a life-long approach, beginning with an integrated strategy to services for disabled children and their families, and then providing opportunities for adults to lead fulfilling lives in their communities. The aim is to bring about improvements across a wide range of services including education, employment, housing and support.

A similarly integrative approach is taken by the 'Supporting People Programme', which was introduced throughout the UK in 2001, but not fully implemented until April 2003. The focus here is on integrating housing services in order to enable 'vulnerable people' to live in the community. In this respect 'vulnerable people' is taken to include not only disabled people but other groups considered to be vulnerable, including older people, women fleeing domestic violence and people with mental health difficulties. Under Supporting People, the funding, planning and commissioning of all housing-related support services has been transferred from housing benefit and the Housing Corporation to local councils, working in partnership with service users, health, probation and support services. The aim is for local authorities and their partners to be able to plan and provide services that are more sensitive to local and individual need, and more accountable and transparent. People with all levels of support needs are potentially eligible for Supporting People funding, which can be combined with other sources of funding into a support package, to enable an individual to live a more independent life in the community.

The Way Ahead

In looking forward, it is possible to identify several recent developments in policy and practice relating to disabled people, which give some positive indicators for the future.

Direct payments

> ...for certain groups true empowerment comes when they have the financial means to arrange their own services, but more importantly the power to influence the range of services available.
>
> (Coulshed and Orme, 1998: 68)

One example of a recent development, which demonstrates the integration of theory and policy in practice, is that of 'Direct Payments'. This idea was introduced through the Community Care (Direct Payments) Act of 1996, which gave local authorities the power, though not the duty, to provide disabled people with the cash to purchase their own community care services. The principle of people being given financial help specifically to enable them to buy in personal and domestic help was introduced in 1988 through the Independent Living Fund. This had a small initial budget, which gave people with severe levels of impairment access to funds to enable them to employ their own support workers, sometimes known as 'personal assistants'. The fact that such payments were made available to disabled people was a landmark in service provision since it gave unprecedented autonomy to those who qualified.

A study by Kestenbaum (1992) found that the arrangements worked well, effecting significant improvements to people's quality of life, as well as helping to prevent admissions to residential care. So popular did the new arrangements prove that demand greatly exceeded government expectations, to the extent that by 1992, the annual budget had risen to £97 million, an amount seen as politically unacceptable. Consequently, the Fund was closed to new applicants during that year, and schemes were set up in conjunction with local authority social work departments instead, but with considerably more restrictive criteria for eligibility.

Direct payments, on the other hand, can be made available to any disabled person (or other eligible person) who has been assessed as needing services, to enable them to purchase their own support. There are many positive outcomes to be derived from such a system. Research by Zarb and Nadash (1994), for example, found that disabled people using this option almost invariably expressed greater satisfaction with the choice and control over their support arrangements and the reliability of provision than those using services. Kestenbaum (1999) found that direct payments packages can open up opportunities for social activity through their flexibility and their acknowledgement of disabled people's aspirations for independent living. Moreover, (Bewley, 2000) argues that direct payments encourage personal growth: 'People start small and as they experience taking control of their own life, they grow in knowledge, ability and confidence.'

Unfortunately, however, there have been problems with the implementation of the system. It has been argued by various organisations and many disabled people themselves that progress has been too slow. Moreover, concern has been expressed about the lack of knowledge and the negative attitudes of some of the council staff working in this area. For example, a team from the Social Services Inspectorate (cited by Snell, 2000), which studied ten local authorities in England, found that, 'most councils and staff still have fully to absorb and carry through independent living philosophy,' and that staff expressed feelings such as anxiety about the 'risks' involved for 'vulnerable people' managing their own services. Nevertheless, a significant and steadily increasing number of people with physical impairments are now receiving direct payments – the total for England in 2002 was 5,459 (Department of Health, 2002) while the total number of direct payments in Scotland in March 2003 was 534 (Scottish Executive, 2004b).

People with learning disabilities, however, have continued to face barriers to accessing direct payments, perhaps best summed up by the Service Users Advisory Group for 'Valuing People' (2001) as 'a reluctance to give Direct Payments to people with learning difficulties' leading to 'rules being made that restricted access rather than supported it'. Some local authorities developed blanket policies that excluded people with learning disabilities from their schemes, largely because of anxieties around complex and contentious issues such as capacity to consent and ability to manage the payment, and the potential for recipients to be exploited by unscrupulous parties. Other authorities were prepared in principle to make direct payments available to people with learning disabilities, but failed to publish accessible information. Such problems are borne out by the statistics, with only 736 people with learning disabilities in receipt of direct payments in England in 2002 (Department of Health, 2002) and fifty-six in Scotland (Direct Payments Scotland, 2002).

There is scope for optimism, however. The Health and Social Care Act 2001 and the subsequent Community Care, Services for Carers and Children's Services (Direct Payments) (England) Regulations (2003) now require local councils to offer direct payments to all individuals who are eligible. The equivalent legislation for Scotland is The Community Care and Health (Scotland) Act 2001. These measures, together with the establishment of the Direct Payments Development Fund in England, signal Governments' intention to extend direct payments to much larger numbers of people. Moreover, they are also taking steps to improve access to direct payments for people who have learning disabilities. Department of Health guidance in 1999 and subsequently has emphasised the importance of accessible information, effective assessment practices, independent support, and flexibility in enabling people to access direct payments. In particular, it is noted that people do not have to manage the money themselves. For example, people with learning disabilities can have the money paid to them via a trust fund. They are allowed to have as much assistance as they require – perhaps from family members, friends, voluntary advocates, or relevant organisations such as Centres for Integrated (or Independent) Living. Another source of support could be a 'service broker' – someone employed specifically to help people plan and organise their support services. Service brokerage has been much discussed in the UK, but is still only practised to any significant extent in North America.

Person-centred planning

The 'person-centred' approach incorporates much of the good practice in social work and care management that we have discussed above, but it also encompasses a 'new vision beyond service based supports and solutions' (Brown, 1999). The concept of person-centred planning has tended to be discussed in relation to people with learning disabilities, but there is no reason why it is not equally applicable to people with physical or sensory impairments. It includes a variety of different techniques such as MAPS, PATHS, Essential Lifestyles Planning and Personal Futures Planning (O'Brien and Lovett, 1992, Small and Harrison,

1992). Each tool aims to involve and empower the individual in making decisions about his/her own life, and focus on that person's attributes and gifts rather than on problems and what they cannot do. Moreover, person-centred planning means seeing the person in the context of their friendships, relationships, family and community connections; their race, ethnicity and religion; their gender and sexuality; their previous experiences and all the other factors that make them who they are. The intention is to enable people to achieve what they really want in their lives, rather than what is dictated by existing service provision.

User involvement in staff recruitment and training

The concept of consulting service users in planning services has already been discussed. This has now extended to user involvement in areas such as staff recruitment and training. It is increasingly being recognised that service users have a right to some say in who supports them, but their involvement in the process of recruiting staff has often been tokenistic, and managers or personnel staff have continued to make the final decisions about whom to appoint. Research carried out by Townsley and Macadam (1996), however, highlighted ways in which disabled people can be involved successfully throughout the staff recruitment process, from drawing up the job description and designing the application form, to selecting the successful candidate and informing all candidates of the final decision. Their study was carried out in relation to day and residential services for people with learning disabilities, but the conclusions are relevant to all services for disabled people. In particular, they found that where service users were involved at every stage in the recruitment process, the outcomes were more likely to be positive for all concerned; that good, appropriate training (including equal opportunities training) was a strong indicator of effective involvement and that planning, practising, and receiving the appropriate level of support were also significant.

Equally, if not more important, is the involvement of disabled people in disability equality training for staff and managers, and in social work education. Oliver and Sapey (1999: 179) argue that training about disability on most social work courses has been both inadequate and inappropriate, 'dominated by theories based on the individual model of disability'. Clearly, the most appropriate people to deliver training that challenges 'disablist' attitudes and assumptions are disabled people themselves. This point was argued strongly by Carol Lee, a member of the People First self-advocacy organisation, speaking at the conference 'Strategies for Quality' held in February 2000 to launch the Government's Learning Disability Training Strategy. While she is referring to people with learning disabilities, her arguments could apply equally to all areas of disability:

> *We are the professionals. Only we know what it is like to have a learning difficulty. All training should include the Social Model of Disability, and*

disability equality training, and people with learning difficulties should do this training... Rather than always taking power and control away from us, staff need to be trained in how to hand the power back to us!

Concluding Comments

So what, then, is the way forward for social work with disabled people? One crucial area is for disabled people themselves to be encouraged into social work training and actively recruited as social workers, not only to redress the discrimination they have so often experienced within employment, but also because of the personal experience and specialist knowledge they can bring to the job. Secondly, it is important to acknowledge that the social work role in this area is changing; indeed in some authorities, there are no longer social workers as such working in the field of disability, only 'care managers'. The role of the social worker/care manager carries inherent contradictions in relation to the community care policies which frontline workers are responsible for implementing on the ground. Stevenson and Parsloe (1993) have demonstrated the importance of high staff morale, of social workers themselves feeling empowered, before they can, in turn, empower others. Such a feeling can be difficult to maintain, however, when social workers, strongly committed to working in a way which empowers disabled people, find themselves in practice limited to assessing needs, rationing resources and with few options to offer people.

Nevertheless, whatever the political and financial climate affecting their day-to-day work, it is important for social workers to hold onto the value base represented by the social model of disability. By working within this model, Oliver and Sapey argue:

The rewards for social workers will arise from the enhanced professional and personal satisfaction that will stem from...the greater potential for achieving change.

(Oliver and Sapey, 1999: 32)

Social workers alone are not responsible for dismantling the barriers that face disabled people; they can, however, give moral and practical support to the process and to disabled people who are fighting for change. In the words of Peter Flynn, the person with a learning disability quoted at the outset: *You need people to believe in you* (Flynn, 1998: 29).

Chapter 6

Social Work and Mental Illness

Kathryn Mackay

Introduction

Social workers will come across mental illness in all client groups. For example depression, the commonest form of mental illness, will affect the ability of the person to carry out day-to-day tasks, whatever the age and circumstances of the person. Research has shown that there is a correlation between maternal depression and the ability to address the various needs of a child (Sheppard, 1999). Depression is often overlooked in an older person due to assumptions about old age (Katona, 1994). The underlying illness, if unrecognised, will not only exacerbate the situation but also reduce the effectiveness of any social work intervention. Therefore, mental illness affects all aspects of social work and is not purely a matter for those who choose to specialise in this area.

It is presently popular to use the term mental health rather than mental illness. The former is seen as more inclusive but it does blur the distinctions that have to be drawn when discussing social work in this field. Someone who is depressed in reaction to a life event may not require any specialised assistance. By contrast, someone with schizophrenia, depending on the severity of the illness and personal factors, may require a range of specialised services over a sustained period of time. This chapter will concentrate on the latter. This is not a homogenous group and the most significant distinction drawn in this chapter is between those who have been long-term hospital patients and those who have recently become service users. Equally, there is no one recognised term for people with mental illness. Depending on their experience, service users may wish to be called just that, others prefer survivor because they see themselves as surviving the psychiatric system whereas the term, consumer, is inappropriate given the power imbalance between users and psychiatric services (Sayce, 2000).

The development of the response of social work to mental illness is inextricably linked to the fundamental changes in NHS psychiatric services that have occurred in the last fifty years. Therefore, the first section of this chapter will briefly review the move from the large hospitals to care in the community, before going on to address social work policy and practice issues. Finally, consideration will be given to future developments in this field. There are challenges in writing about social work and mental illness in the United Kingdom because England and Wales, Northern Ireland and Scotland have their own legal and policy frameworks. Devolution for Wales and Scotland since 1999 has added to the complexity. The cultural and geographical differences across Britain should also not be underplayed. In isolated communities, the alternatives to hospital will be more restrictive than those available in the bigger population centres. The writer, being based in Scotland, will refer to Scottish law and policy in explaining the social work response to mental illness and draw on her own practice experience as well as relevant literature.

From Hospital to Community Care

There have been vast changes in the way NHS psychiatric services have been delivered over the last thirty years. A range of inter-related factors lay behind the move towards community care such as societal views, critical research, government policy, improvements in treatment and the financial cost of maintaining hospitals (Rogers and Pilgrim, 1996). The purpose of this section is to consider how far community care has progressed for people who are mentally ill. As such, it is necessary to briefly remind the reader of the conditions in the psychiatric hospitals as many of their former patients continue to receive services today.

The traditional psychiatric hospitals were mainly built at a distance from urban areas and held upwards of 2000 people. Some patients were not mentally ill at all and those who were may not have been severely ill. Family circumstances and inclination of individual doctors were significant in whether a person would end up being a long- term patient. Patients lived on large open wards with very little privacy and staff were often poorly trained. As a result, maltreatment and abuse by other patients and staff was not uncommon. The process of institutionalisation also had impact, in for example moulding people into model patients (Goffman, 1961). It is not surprising that people who experienced these environments often have a deep mistrust of psychiatric services. It is also the case that many of the present day nurses and doctors worked in these hospitals and this is one of many reasons behind the view that psychiatric practice itself may not be so very different today (Clarke, 1999; Sayce 2000). A study conducted in the late 1980s of Social Work and Community Psychiatric Nurse (CPN) practice within a Community Mental Health Team (CMHT) supported the view that CPNs continued to work within a medical framework (Shepperd, 1991).

The first major policy initiative to run down the large hospitals was taken in 1962 when Enoch Powell announced his Hospital Plan. This aimed to halve the number of psychiatric hospital beds in fifteen years, focus future care around general hospitals and create community resources (Sheppard, 1991). However, in 1986, a government report highlighted the continued dearth of community resources and the gross imbalance in funding in favour of hospital based services.

Even now though the balance of service provision may have drastically altered, the financial imbalance still exists. In 1999/98 the total mental illness budget for health and social work in Scotland was over £320 million. Four fifths of that was spent by the NHS, and within the NHS budget, 78% was spent on inpatient services (Accounts Commission for Scotland, 1999). This has led the Accounts Commission for Scotland to state that, 'Current expenditure does not appear to be matched to need and is still more likely to reflect historical patterns of expenditure' (Accounts Commission for Scotland 1999: 1). This tension between local authorities and the NHS is still the most significant block to effective working (Accounts Commission for Scotland, 1999; Rogers and Pilgrim, 1996).

There have been few evaluations of the move from hospital to community care. However, one stands out for the studies length of duration and depth of analysis (Leff et al., 1997). The evaluation monitored and reviewed the outcomes of the closure programmes of two hospitals in London and concluded:

- Community care does work for all but a very small minority of patients.
- Good quality community care is not cheaper than hospital care for those with a severe and enduring illness.
- Those placed in smaller residential units had more quality of life than those in larger nursing homes and that a range of accommodation services was required to suit varying needs.
- The concentration on the discharge of long stay hospital patients had been made at the expense of the needs of those already in the community requiring psychiatric services.
- Little progress has been made in the employment of ex-patients and meaningful activities outside the home are limited.
- Integration within and acceptance by the local community was limited.

(Leff et al.,1997)

It is important to note that the number of hospital admissions has dramatically risen as the number of hospital beds has reduced (Raftery, 1997). There has also been a corresponding increase in the use of the Mental Health (Scotland) Act 1984 to admit compulsorily people to hospital (Mental Welfare Commission for Scotland, 1998). There are a number of factors behind these statistics. For example, admissions have increased due to new categories of treatable problems such as depression, personality disorders and substance misuse (Raftery, 1997). The reasons for re-admissions are more complex and inter-related: there are less hospital beds, hospital stays are shorter and the emphasis is on getting people discharged as soon as possible. The problem here is that the person may not be sufficiently recovered and community services not responsive enough to give the optimum chance of full recovery (Leff et al., 1997). The danger is that the person will become a revolving door patient caught in a regular cycle of admission, discharge and readmission.

The increased use of legislation may also be an indicator of the continued unease about mental illness expressed by the community. This is supported by the Leff et al. (1997) study, which found community care had progressed only in so far as where people lived and there was limited wider integration. In summary, although NHS provision has moved from large-scale hospitals to small inpatient units, day hospitals and CMHTs, there is still an underlying hospital based approach to managing mental illness.

The Developing Role of Social Work Alongside Psychiatric Services

Social Work Services have varied in their level of involvement with the NHS psychiatric services, and generally, partnerships were forged at practitioner rather than management level until well into the 1990s. For example, CMHTs were established by the NHS psychiatric services from the 1970s onwards. Their aim was to reduce the need for hospitalisation by responding more quickly to referrals with community based options for treatment. In some CMHTs, social workers may have had a full time presence and contributed to its daily work, management and development. In others, social workers would only be attached on a sessional basis or there may well have been no social work presence at all. However, there was evidence that the nature of the relationship between individual social workers and psychiatric services was significant in determining the outcome for service users (Connor, 1999; Huxley, 1985).

The NHS and Community Care 1990, hereafter referred to as the 1990 Act, was significant in a number of ways for frontline workers, managers and planners. It was the starting point for more formalised relationships, at all levels, between local authorities and the NHS psychiatric services; an agenda which more recent legislative changes have moved forward. The 1990 Act introduced the 'purchaser/provider' concept to the NHS and to local authorities. In theory, social workers would assess people's needs and then secure services to meet those needs from within their own organisation or from independent providers. The implications of the 1990 Act in relation to older people were discussed in Chapter three and this chapter will look at its specific relevance to the development of mental health services.

Firstly, the 1990 Act heralded the introduction of 'care management' which challenged one of the fundamental roles of social workers in this field, that of ongoing support and counselling. Care management by its name does not preclude traditional social work practice but it has become associated with such a move in Britain (Sturges, 1996). There are several models of care management and for example, it can be a task undertaken as part of the social work role within a CMHT. Those who are part of generic community care teams are often under more pressure to confine their role to an administrative model of care management, (minimal intervention in completing an assessment form and referral on to services), due to the pressure of referral rates and budget restrictions. Care management as a concept is also unpopular with service users due to its inherent assumption that people who require care also need to be managed (Sayce, 2000). These issues were discussed further in respect of people with disabilities in Chapter five.

Secondly, the 1990 Act transferred funding for residential and nursing home care in the private and voluntary sector, from the DSS with its unlimited budget, to the local authorities who had tight financial constraints. This new gate keeping responsibility for assessing and paying for residential care created more interdisciplinary conflict. Some psychiatrists had been proactive in discharging patients to nursing and residential homes without much recourse to social workers. They now found that they had to wait for assessments to be completed and funding to be agreed before the person could be discharged. This became a slow process depending on referral waiting lists, the level of autonomy the workers were given and where the budget was sited within the Social Work Departments. This tension between the psychiatrists and the social work services continues today.

This same community care budget was to be used to stimulate developments in the independent sector, so as to broaden the range of services available. Local authorities however, were not equipped to do this on such a large scale (Lewis and Glennerster, 1996). Those leaving hospital and requiring some form of residential care took, and continue to take, the greatest proportion of the budget. As such, the general trend was that local authorities followed the NHS path of change; concentrating on those with established long term needs at the expense of those who were at risk of losing their place in the community.

Thirdly, previous government reports had called for more effective communication and planning between the NHS and Local Authorities at all levels. The 1990 Act took this a step further by introducing local Community Care plans. These had to state the nature of current provision and intended future developments. This placed Social Work Services in a pivotal position for planning mental health services for the first time. However, as noted above the funding is still heavily balanced in favour of NHS inpatient care. Further governmental initiatives in the 1990s have tried to urge this process on, for example, the Framework for Mental Health Services in Scotland (Scottish Office, 1997). The Care Programme Approach (CPA) is another example: it is a shared system of assessment, management and review for people with severe and enduring illness, with either the local authority or the NHS Trust taking the lead in the overall management of the system (Scottish Office, 1996).

Fourthly, the 1990 Act created local authority registration and inspection units, which have now been replaced by the national Care Commission in Scotland and the Care Standards Commission in England. There are now explicit standards for care. In Scotland, these have been written from the viewpoint of services users and their families, with underlying principles such as respect for the individual, and a focus on issues such as exercise of choice and decision-making.

Finally, the 1990 Act introduced one specific measure for mental illness: mental illness specific grants to stimulate new resources, particularly in the voluntary sector. The local authorities were given the lead in applying for these grants from a central fund and they were seen as a largely positive development (McCollam, 1999). They have created a range of innovative community based supports such as counselling services, day and respite care and employment schemes. However, the funding for some of the projects is not financially secure and this raises issues of sustainability (McCollam, 1999).

The Community Care and Health (Scotland) Act 2002 formalised the Joint Future Agenda (Scottish Executive, 2000) which has been the latest policy initiative to expand joint agency working at both the managerial and practitioner level. This Act aims to remove the barriers to joint working that have always existed but only tinkered with in the past. It represents a fundamental structural and procedural change that will affect all workers in the community care field. The Act allows for health and social work to manage services on behalf of the other. For example, social workers could be placed more firmly within CMHTs. Alternatively, home support and rehabilitation budgets could be pooled together under one service. The only functions that cannot be delegated to the NHS from local authorities are those of the mental health officer and these will be discussed later in the chapter. Similar initiatives have been introduced in England and Wales.

In summary the local authority social work role has expanded at all levels, with many shared functions now being formalised. There is sustained interaction with the NHS PHCTs and private and voluntary sectors to create more appropriate services. However, local authorities like the NHS PHCTs face the seemingly impossible task of meeting the needs of those with severe and enduring mental illness as well as providing more preventative services for those who have recently experienced mental illness. The next section will continue to look at this tension as it considers the impact of the above changes on the day-to-day work with service users.

It should be noted, however, that increasingly sustained work with mental health service users is being carried out by voluntary organisations. These organisations, particularly in large urban areas, are able offer advice, support, housing and advocacy. They are also more likely to be co-managed and delivered by services users themselves and are therefore seen as more empowering services (Barnes and Bowl, 2001).

Social Work Practice Today

Mental health social work practice has received little attention by researchers and evidence of the effectiveness of practice remains anecdotal (Fisher et al., 1984;

Ulas and Connor, 1999). Core social work skills such as relationship building, assessment, support, counselling and networking are required. On top of this, effective social work intervention also requires more specialist knowledge and therapeutic skills due to the very nature of mental illness (Fisher et al., 1984; Huxley, 1985). The Sheppard study (1991) provides a good overview of the role:

> Social workers defined their client primarily in terms of social problems, where mental health case definitions received a higher profile amongst CPNs. Social workers, according to the main indicators-role, context and indirect work-operated in a wider community context than CPNs. Social workers acted as advocate or resource mobilisers, worked with outside agencies and professionals, and tackled more practical and emotional and relationship problems indirectly to a far greater extent than CPNs.
>
> (Sheppard, 1991: 75)

The study also recorded higher satisfaction levels with social work from the service users. On a practical note, nurses are ward, unit or community based, whereas social workers can remain involved through the whole process of admission, in-patient care and post discharge. Therefore, the role of the social worker continues to be a distinct and valuable one. The rest of this section will describe the key tasks in more detail.

Assessment and establishing the worker/person relationship

The assessment and intervention framework used by social workers can best be described as a bio-psychosocial model; it recognises that mental illness is caused and aggravated by a range of personal and environmental factors as well as physiological factors (Huxley, 1985). For example a young woman, who had been in a secure psychiatric hospital prior to moving to a local unit, disclosed a medical condition for the first time to a social work student. A surgical operation completely cured the problem and this had a positive impact on her self-esteem and mental health. It was the more empowering relationship created by the social worker that was significant in the woman having the courage to tell someone about a physical problem that predated the mental illness.

Where the person with mental illness is from an ethnic minority, workers presumptions can be doubly discriminatory, with crude stereotypes regarding their needs and the level of family support available (Watters, 1996). An example from the author's experience provides an illustration. A young black woman, who was resident in a secure hospital, was the subject of racist taunts, which the staff did not recognise as an issue because those who were making the taunts were mentally ill. The woman's confusion about her identity was seen as part of her illness and again staff failed to recognise this as an issue, in its own right.

The recovery from mental illness is an uneven and unpredictable path. Effective social work requires a relationship to be built up and this may take some time to establish. It is crucial not to ignore the impact of the illness itself. Social workers, in the writers experience, can underestimate the effect illness has on interpersonal communication. For example, depression can make people withdraw into themselves. Similarly, those who hear voices, may have those voices competing with the worker's dialogue. As a result, workers might see the person as uncooperative or gain limited information. Because of the illness itself, or through anxiety over how the worker may respond, the person might not be able to voice their difficulties in speaking. As a result, a proper assessment will not take place. The views of other professionals, family and friends might supply valuable information but it is has to be remembered that this is from their individual perspective and cannot replace the person's own views.

Decisions should never to be made when a person is unwell and usually a holding situation can be achieved. For example, single people admitted to hospital are sometimes put under pressure to give up their own homes in favour of supported accommodation. The social worker's role here is to advocate for no action to be taken. Once a person gives up their home they are effectively homeless and the decision is irreversible. In this situation, social workers can liaise with the housing agency where eviction and disrepair may be a possibility. Although there are legal systems in place to make decisions for an individual who is mentally incapacitated, the present methods are unacceptable because they cannot deal with a specific issue without taking decision making away from the person. Scotland has taken the lead in Britain in modernising this legislation, through the Adults with Incapacity (Scotland) Act 2000, which established principles and systems to minimise any legal intervention. The Act gives a greater focus to the individual, the ability of relatives or carers to take action without recourse to court and where the courts are required that interventions will be based on the person's needs and not a prescribed list of powers.

It is also important that where support is offered it is not withdrawn too quickly, particularly where there is no positive family or social network in place. Social work intervention is much more effective when available to help someone over a bad patch, rather than place them back on the waiting list, only to pick up the pieces when someone has become ill again (Howe, 1998). Therefore, the time limits that are sometimes set for assessment and care management are inappropriate for many people with mental illness.

Advocacy

Social work textbooks see advocacy as a core requirement of social work, particularly in relation to learning disability, which was discussed in chapter five, and mental health (Payne, 1991). However, advocacy does require the worker to be knowledgeable about the issue they are challenging, to have the motivation to persist with the issue, and to have a manager who values such activities and will support them when necessary. Advocacy is seen increasingly by pressure groups as an activity, which only voluntary agencies should fulfil. There are a range of models in use including self, group and professional advocacy (Henderson and Pochin, 2001).

The writer will provide an example from her own experience to show why independent advocacy can be necessary at times. A man who had been discharged from hospital with home support had his care package reviewed by the local community care team and it was decided that home support was no longer necessary. Whilst working with this man, a number of issues became apparent. Firstly, the care manager undertaking the review was a victim of poor communication, receiving few details from the team at the hospital who set up the care package. However, the care manager seemed to mistrust inherently others involved to provide the missing information. Secondly, the care manager was working from a service led perspective, which was about preservation of the budget rather than the needs of the client. Although the man's care package did come to an end, advocacy ensured that his diagnosis and needs were accepted as valid and recorded. In addition, a tailoring off period, rather than an abrupt end to home support was secured. This should have been standard practice but had been overlooked in the push to save money.

Occasionally advocacy can lead to conflict within the social work department. This is often at its most clear when service users are also parents and their children are clients of children and families teams. Clearly, a small minority of children will require protection as a result of parental mental illness. Equally, children can become carers for their parents, which may in turn affect their welfare (Becker et al., 1998). There is a tension between the rights of the mentally ill person to be a parent and the rights of the child to have a 'good enough' parent, and any resulting social work intervention has been described by Sue White as the 'poisoned chalice' (White, 1996). For example, a mother with schizophrenia who was struggling to cope but who was accepting help from her family and social worker, had her baby's name placed on the child protection register. If the mother had not been co-operating with professionals or the child had been harmed in some way, the act of registration would have been more meaningful. In accepting help, this mother had laid herself open to extra scrutiny and stress, which might have made her less able to cope.

Education

Social workers not only need to know about mental illness, interventions and services but they also need to be able to impart this knowledge to others. The recipient of information may be the service user themselves, their family or other workers involved in providing care. There is a lot that people can do individually to live more successfully with mental illness. For example, an older woman was admitted to hospital after living successfully in a group home for five years. She became ill again with a schizophrenic illness after stopping her medication. In discussion with the woman, it became clear she had never been told she had a mental illness let alone schizophrenia. Through some basic work by the CPN and the writer, the woman chose to remain on medication. The distress caused by the re-emergence of the symptoms and the forced admission to hospital were a result of failure by previous staff to accord this woman respect and credit her with the ability to make rational choices.

The bulk of support for someone with mental illness continues to come from his or her family and friends. Although some service users will have poor relationships with their families, the vast majority will have positive family experiences and it is the worker's responsibility to facilitate family involvement. The rule of confidentiality will apply in that such contact is with the person's express consent or that they are present. There are only two instances where this should be breached: when it is a legal requirement or where someone is at significant risk. Relatives frequently complain that they have been ignored when they attempted to obtain help for someone who was mentally ill and that later when the person was discharged; they were not made part of the planning process (Howe, 1998). Carers' rights to involvement in care planning have increased due the Health and Community Care (Scotland) Act 2002.

Relatives identify a number of factors, which are helpful: a general practitioner who is responsive and spends time with them, information about the person's illness and advice about how they might help and workers, however qualified, who will quickly respond if the person's health starts to deteriorate (Howe, 1998).

Despite financial restrictions and the lack of expertise in local authorities, new resources have been developed in the independent sector. Today, in the cities and larger urban areas, there are many specialist agencies that provide a good standard of care. By contrast, rural areas cannot sustain specialist services. The social worker then has to take on an educational and support role for those providing care. For example, home carers who primarily 'look after' older people may find it difficult to work alongside a younger person in doing the shopping and housework together. They may disapprove of what they see as laziness but lack of volition can be caused by the illness itself or can be a side effect of medication.

Counselling

Often more therapeutic work needs to be undertaken to enable the person to improve their ability to cope with stress and find ways to protect themselves from recurring mental illness. Obviously, other professionals can perform this role and contact with other service users can be invaluable in gaining support and finding out how others cope. However it is the writers experience, that where effective relationships have been established at a time of crisis, service users may prefer to remain with the same worker rather than go to a different service (Huxley, 1984). This is where educational work can merge into general counselling; allowing the person time to express their thoughts and discuss their view of the future. The social worker needs to have the ability to work in partnership with the person to tackle anxiety and doubt and to help the person find the right balance between making progress and placing too much stress, too quickly upon themselves.

Childhood neglect and abuse are significant factors in adults who experience mental illness. It has been estimated that half the women receiving psychiatric services have experienced sexual or physical abuse (Holmshaw and Hillier, 2000). Relationship problems can also be significant in a person's illness and recovery. Social workers, with appropriate knowledge and skills, can undertake more specialised forms of counselling. There are discrete services for people who have been sexually abused or who have relationship problems but there will be times when this is not an option for the person. Again, the nature of the mental illness may require the more specialist knowledge of a mental health social worker in adjusting the work to the needs of that person.

Risk

Risk assessment and management receives a high profile in mental health work today but it is important to note that risk and dangerousness are separate concepts. The vast majority of people with mental illness do not pose a risk to others, but they themselves are placed at risk of institutionalisation, unemployment, poverty, homelessness and stigma both by the services who aim to help and by the community at large. Therefore, for most service users, intervention should be aimed at retaining or improving a person's quality of life and not just on stabilising and monitoring.

There is a strong link between mental health and self-harm and suicide (Langan, 2000). The extent to which one person may be more at risk than another is complex. For example, there are differences based on gender in that women are more likely to seek help, their suicide attempts less successful and the method less violent than men (Vassilas and Morgan, 1997). There are also other factors such as childhood abuse that make this behaviour more likely. For the social worker, knowledge of risk factors pertinent to the person's age and situation is necessary in order to assess the degree of risk (Blumental, 1990).

There is a very small minority of people who do pose a danger to others when ill and they do require intensive support and close supervision. However, it should be noted that the link between mental illness and violence is complicated and that substance abuse is also a significant factor (Langan, 2000). Influence of societal perceptions is particularly evident in this arena. For example, Afro-Caribbean people are substantially over-represented in those people who are removed to hospital under mental health legislation, from public places, by the police: thirty-nine per cent as opposed to eighteen per cent in the population (Rogers, 1990). This study highlighted the 'crucial role played by the public in setting the agenda for subsequent police action' (Rogers, 1990: 233).

The management of risk requires a network of support in which each person is clear about their role and the risk indicators for that particular person (Blumental, 1990; Ryan, 1997). Daily contacts can help to identify critical changes in presentation and routine that indicate the person may be entering a period when they are more at risk. For example, through regular contact with a woman who had a history of self-harm and serious suicide attempts, alongside liaison with her psychiatrist, it became possible to predict more easily when she was at risk. Certain forms of self-harm the woman inflicted on herself were not dangerous. For example, she superficially lacerated her arms. Although work was carried out to assist the woman to use less destructive means to relieve stress, she had done this for many years and it was part of her coping mechanism. However, when she began to isolate herself from those around her and voice delusional thoughts, she was more likely to make a suicide attempt. Careful monitoring by the staff involved achieved, over time, a large reduction in the more damaging suicide attempts and a consequent reduction in hospital admissions, by increasing support during critical phases of her illness.

In recent years, there have been a number of murders committed by mentally ill people. They have received widespread attention, with health and local authorities being condemned for their failure to protect the public (Howlett, 1997). Clearly much has been learnt about how to reduce the possibility of such incidents. The Care Programme Approach has helped to improve co-ordination and shared responsibility for vulnerable people across agencies. The danger exists however that where there are formal frameworks to manage risk, they are used too readily. Although there is little evidence yet that this is the case with CPA, it is interesting to note that based on practice experience rather than research, older people with dementia are less likely to be referred than those who are younger and are seen to pose a risk to others. It is also important to stress that risk assessment and management can be carried out within an informal network such as the one described above. Just as other areas of social work operate a tariff system of informal through to statutory intervention for people who are vulnerable, so responses to mental illness should aim to provide effective services with the minimum amount of formal intervention.

Multi-disciplinary work

It will be clear by now that multi-disciplinary work is an essential activity of social workers. The previous sections have all referred to the need to work closely with other agencies. The productiveness of such relationships may depend as much on individual personalities and motivations as the formal systems that may be in place (Øvretveit, 1993). The medical profession, especially, do not respect social work as a profession so much as the individual (Buckley, 1997). Multi-disciplinary work is obviously easier if the social worker is part of the CMHTs where their influence is noted not only on intervention but also on the working of the team (Huxley, 1985). However, for community care teams the GPs are often the first point of contact. Multi-disciplinary work can be left in place when a situation requires it, but this rarely leads to an overall improvement in the relationship, and a more proactive approach can have better results. For example, the investment of time given to attend regularly the local GP meeting can bring about better referrals in both directions, a shared sense of priorities for the local community and support at times of crises for the worker. Front line workers share a common concern, the person with the mental illness and positive working relationships enable agreement on a shared way forward. Effective work requires not only structures that enable joint working to take place but a willingness from individual workers to open up their own practice for scrutiny by other professionals.

Approved Mental Health Officer

Social Work has one specific role with mentally ill people that is set in legislation, through the provision of Mental Health Officers (MHOs) (Approved Social Worker [ASW] in England.). MHOs are experienced social workers who receive extra training and are then assessed to carry out functions under mental health legislation. Both Scotland and England and Wales have new Acts of Parliament that will, it is argued, modernise legal intervention regarding mental illness. There will be a continuing number of differences in the context in which MHOs and ASWs perform their similar functions, but these cannot be detailed here. One key difference that is important to note is that in Scotland the MHO functions will continue to be carried out only by social workers and not other mental health professionals as proposed in England and Wales.

The Mental Health (Care and Treatment) (Scotland) Act 2003 confirms and expands the role of the MHO, which are as follows:

- To consider giving consent to a patient's forced admission to hospital.
- Make applications for the longer term to the Mental Health Tribunal for compulsory Treatment Order (to detain a person in hospital or provide treatment in the community).
- Preparation of a care plan where there is an application for a compulsory treatment order where the person will remain living in the community.
- Preparation of social circumstances reports on patients who are subject to compulsory intervention.
- Provision of advice to people who are subject to compulsory intervention and their carers on legal and administrative procedures.
- Application for and supervision of certain guardianship and intervention orders.

The role of the MHO initially developed in the 1980s after research into practice under the previous legislation revealed that GPs and social workers in particular had a poor grasp of the law (Bean, 1980). Psychiatrists though less uninformed still carried out interventions that were not within the letter of the law. The MHO role was seen as offering an independent view as to whether hospitalisation was necessary and ensuring it was carried out properly (Campbell and Heginbotham, 1991). This was formal recognition of what social work at its best could offer: assessment, advice and advocacy. As a result, MHOs need to keep up to date with legislation and policy. They also need to conduct themselves competently in a court of law. Most importantly, although they are not experts on mental illness, they need to be able to balance the control and treatment with the person's right to live the way they wish and not to have their liberty taken away.

Future challenges

It will be clear by now that the social work response to mental illness involves tensions that have existed for many years and indeed will continue to be focus of the future challenges. These include individual freedom versus state control, the imbalance between NHS and local authority finances, the restrictions of the care management model and the extent to which community care means more than the address at which a person lives. There is no doubt that the future development of social work will continue to be intertwined with that of NHS psychiatric services. Central government has been increasingly influential in setting the local agenda for both agencies and will continue to do so. This section only has space to cover some of the key national issues.

Recent legislation has introduced the concept of enforcement treatment in the community, which raises civil rights issues and exemplifies the continued tension between individual rights and the perceived protection of others. There has always been a propensity, as noted above, for cautious professionals to use methods of intervention when they are not necessary and these new powers are of concern to many service users and their organisations (Ferguson, 2003).

The present financial and political environment means that both local authorities and the NHS are struggling to cope with the overwhelming demand for mental health services. The focus on those who have been long-term patients and those with severe and enduring mental illness may only be of short- term benefit. Those who are beginning to experience mental illness may become long-term patients or enter homelessness in the future (Leff et al., 1997; Lipscombe, 1997). Services are presently struggling to meet this wider range of needs. Some way has to be found to carry out more preventative work that allows workers to support people on an ongoing basis. Services need to focus on issues around employment as well as fundamental needs such as housing and finances. The voluntary sector can only presently fulfil this role to a limited extent, due to its precarious funding and need to work within stated priority areas.

Joint working continues to improve slowly. Whether the rest of Britain follows the example of Northern Ireland and merges social work with health services is a matter of conjecture. Workers are generally happy with the idea of social work services and primary health care staff sharing offices but they are less comfortable with being employed by the PHCT or vice versa. Given the adversarial role which social work at times is required to take, one can understand the need for independence. On the other hand, it might help finally to break down the barriers set up around budgets and services.

It is clear that social work has a range of responsibilities for people with mental illness, from individual work by social workers and MHOs to overall service provision, planning and quality assurance. However, this remit is being increasingly restricted to those with severe and enduring mental illness and this is hindering more preventative work taking place, whether that be directly by social workers themselves or commissioned from a voluntary agency. The final words of this chapter will therefore be from one who sees the term of 'institution in the community' as indicative of where all services are presently stuck:

Institution in the community implies that community mental health services would be acceptable if only they would cease to resemble institutions...This is a limited goal. It fails to set as an aim changes in the whole social environment, which would break down the barriers of exclusion from economic and social life. It fails to require that one role of mental health services should be to facilitate social inclusion.

(Sayce, 2000: 81)

Chapter 7

Future Developments in Social Work

Steven M Shardlow

Both the past and the future are mysterious places; the past we romanticise as a place where things were done differently; the future we idealise as a place where dreams may come true – either as the fulfilment of treasured wishes or nightmares. Yet the future is ultimately unknowable, although as Albert Einstein commented that he never thought of the future as it came soon enough[1]! Attempts to peer into the future are notoriously fraught with difficulty and can even be dangerous as Cassandra discovered with her prophesies in ancient Greece. It maybe difficult, well nigh impossible even to look tentatively into the future before it happens, but it is fun to speculate and to try to see what might be in store for us, either personally or professionally.

Despite the difficulties with gazing into the future there are some informed judgements that can be made based upon trends that are evident at present.

It is probably true to state that the similarities in the way that social work is practised in the various countries of the United Kingdom are currently stronger than are the differences. However, there are emerging trends that suggest that this state of affairs may not continue indefinitely. The process of devolving political power, set in train by the creation of the Scottish Parliament and Welsh Assembly has created separate institutions, which are concerned with social work in each of the differing countries of the UK. These institutions build upon what were different traditions and practices – even, as in the case of Scotland, a different legal system. We might ask how different is social work in these countries – how different might it become – and how might it affect the lives of people who use social work. Perhaps two of the most obvious differences can be found in Scotland (i.e. where Scotland differs most from the other countries in the United Kingdom) these concern the experience of young offenders and older people. In respect of young offenders there is in Scotland a judicial structure known as the Children's Panel. Here in a relatively informal atmosphere there is an attempt to understand the young persons actions in a non-adversarial environment. Whilst a young person

---

[1] Comment made in an interview given on the *Belgenland*, December 1930.

attending a Children's Panel will undoubtedly experience the event as a formal part of the legal process it will not have the same character as the court hearings that young people may have to face elsewhere in the United Kingdom. In respect of older people, Scotland provides care for older people at either no cost or a much reduced cost. This may result in older people being more willing to accept care when they are in need. There are many other significant differences across the four countries of the UK. These tend to be concerned with organisational structures as a growing sense of national identity becomes a factor in the development of different forms of social work (Payne and Shardlow, 2002). Looking to the future, we might reasonably expect that as powers are devolved to the various countries that greater and more divergent social work practices will emerge.

If you are considering a career in social work and intend to enter a course leading to a professional qualification in social work, then one area of growing difference concerns social work education in the four countries. Details of these differences are to be found on the websites of organisations listed in *Useful Websites* section at the end of the book.

At an organisational level, there are major shifts in evidence that are likely to continue to affect social work across the United Kingdom. During the past ten years, there has been an enormous growth in the number of private and voluntary social work organisations. Such that now, and precise figures are difficult to obtain, over half of all employed social workers are to be found in the private and voluntary sectors rather than working for the local authority, which had previously been the largest provider of care and services in the formal sector. (It should never be forgotten that the majority of care is provided within and by the family and other local networks.) Therefore, newly qualifying social workers are more likely to find employment in the private and voluntary sector than ever before. Other equally dramatic changes are taking place in the organisational landscape of social work. Social workers are increasingly likely to work in multidisciplinary teams within a multi-agency working environment. A good example being the Youth Offending Teams (YOTs) set up by Crime and Disorder Act 1998 or the Community Mental Health Teams (CMHTs) which have existed for longer. There is more evidence of joint organisational arrangements being set up especially between health services and social care/social work. Here again, there are significant differences across the United Kingdom. For example, Northern Ireland has, for many years had a system of joint Boards, which have been responsible for both health and social care. With the prospect of greater integration of health and social care, across the UK, it is therefore even more important for social workers to be able to work in multi-disciplinary teams and to be able to understand the nature of collaborative practice. It is highly likely that these trends will develop and strengthen.

Government policy towards the public services has in recent years emphasised the importance of measuring levels of performance by particular organisations. This has happened in respect of education and health with the publication of so called 'league tables'. In 2002, the same policy initiative was first introduced in respect of local authorities with the publication of the 'star' system: whereby each local authority social services department was awarded either three, two, one or no stars depending upon measured performance particularly against some fifty key performance indicators. This has implications for the way that organisations behave, in that the meeting of pre-defined targets may assume paramount importance. The longer-term implications of such a system are unclear; however, there is considerable pressure for those local authorities without a star to seek ways to improve measured performance. In addition, job prospects for senior managers are likely to be affected (some have lost their jobs on account of poor performance). At practitioner level, the importance of meeting key targets is also likely to be felt with pressure to respond to organisation need rather than necessarily meeting the immediate expectations of service users. It can be hard to measure social work using quantitative indicators, as a respondent in a recent research study commented[2]:

> *And it's hard in quantitative terms, to measure things like the nature and the quality of relationships between practitioners and young people for instance, how do you measure, the sort of level of the exchanges, you know the good relationships, things like empathy and trust and warmth and openness, respect and courtesy and all those kinds of things. They play an enormous part in helping service users, clients to move on and feel good about themselves and those kinds of things, and I think it's those things that we struggle with really.*

These are very real pressures and tensions and ones that are likely to have even more impact in the future.

Another major development that is just about to take effect and will impact upon the nature of social work is the requirement that to become a *social worker* (as of 1 April 2005) it will be necessary to register with one of the Care Councils (depending upon in which country of the United Kingdom the person happens to live). In future, it will not be possible to state that you are a *social worker* unless you are registered. This should provide service users with greater confidence about the education and expertise of those who seek to provide help. It should also provide a mechanism to ensure that those unsuitable do not practice social work.

One of the most significant changes that is taking place and is likely to continue is the development of more knowledge about social work that has been derived from research – especially knowledge about what does or does not work in the delivery of services. Knowledge about good practice has been particularly derived from practice experience, service user opinions and evidence derived from research. The growth in importance of evidence about good practice is especially significant,

---

[2] This is from a research study conducted in a Northern city by Salford Centre for Social Work Research.

such that Sheldon and Chilvers (2000), drawing on the work of Sackett et al. (1996) offer the following definition:

Evidence-based social care is the conscientious, explicit and judicious use of current best evidence in making decisions regarding the welfare of those in need. (p 5)

Evidence-based approaches to the delivery of social work have assumed increasing importance as the government seeks to *modernise* social work and social care. This emphasis is likely to assume an ever more significant contribution in the practice of social work as attempts are made to codify knowledge through the actions of bodies such as SCIE (Social Care Institute for Excellence)[3].

Linked to the growth in importance of evidence based practice for social work is the increased use of information technology by social workers (at the end of the book some useful websites have been included). Social work must always remain a quintessentially human activity where the primary mode of action for social workers lies in the interaction between the service user, carer and the social worker. New technologies can help and they can increase efficiency but they must not be allowed to intervene in the core elements of good social work practice. To promote and enhance the quality of that relationship it will be essential for social workers to seek to develop, in partnership with service users and carers new and better ways of working together to promote the interests of all those who use social work.

In looking toward the future we should be optimistic about the future of social work. Although the forms of providing social help have changed greatly in the past 125 years or so (the late nineteenth-century can be taken as a convenient point to mark the birthplace of modern *'social work'* – it was the period when the words *social work* were first used) it will, no doubt continue to evolve and change. We can be sure that some of the challenges identified in this book will remain. Social work is likely to have to grapple with tensions implicit in providing care for those unable to care for themselves for whatever reason and to protect some sections of society both from themselves and others. These two sets of responsibilities do not sit easily together – it is unlikely that they ever will. Similarly, social work as a discipline will always find itself located at the intersection between the interests of service users and carers balanced against those of employers and social workers themselves. The voice of the service user and carer should be paramount but these are not the only voices to be heard,

Whether you have just joined social work, are thinking about becoming a social worker, or have been working in practice for some time, working on these challenges is the stuff of good social work practice.

---

[3] SCIE operates in respect of England and Wales and at the time of writing, there are negations about SCIE's role in respect of Northern Ireland. Scotland has separate arrangements.

Bibliography

Accounts Commission for Scotland (1999) *A Shared Approach, Developing Adult Mental Health Services*, Edinburgh: Accounts Commission for Scotland.

Adams, R., Dominelli, L. and Payne, M. (eds) (1998) *Social Work: Themes, Issues and Critical Debates*, Basingstoke: Macmillan.

Adcock, M. (2002) 'Assessment', in Wilson, K. and James, A. (eds) *The Child Protection Handbook*. 2nd edn, London: Balliere Tindall. 253–71.

Ahmad, B. (1993) *Black Perspectives in Social Work*, Birmingham: Venture Press.

Allen I., Hogg, D. and Pearce, S. (1992) *Elderly People: Choice, Participation and Satisfaction*, London, Policy Studies Institute.

Annis, L.V., Mathers, L.G. and Baker, C.A. (1984) 'Victim Workers as Therapists for Incarcerated Sex Offenders', *Victimology* 9: 3/4, 426–35.

Arber, S. and Ginn, J. (1991) *Gender and Later Life*, London: Sage.

Arber, S. and Ginn, J. (1996) *Connecting Gender to Ageing: A Sociological Approach*. Buckingham: Open University Press.

Association of Directors of Social Work (1997) *Social Work into the Millennium. A Report by ADSW on Critical Issues for Social Work Services in Scotland*, Scotland: ADSW.

Audit Commission (1986) *Making a Reality of Community Care*, London: HMSO.

Audit Commission (1994) *Seen but not Heard*, London: HMSO.

Audit Commission (1997) *The Coming of Age: Improving Care Services for Older People*, London: HMSO.

Bailey, R. (1995) 'Helping Offenders as an Element in Justice', in Ward, D. and Lacey, M. (eds) *Probation: Working for Justice*, London: Whiting and Birch. 127–39.

Bailey, R. and Brake, M. (1975) *Radical Social Work*, London: Edward Arnold.

Baldwin, S. and Lunt, N. (1996) *Charging Ahead: The Development of Local Authority Charging Policies for Community Care*, Bristol: The Policy Press.

Bank-Mikkelson, N. (1980) 'Denmark', in Flynn, R.J. and Nitsch, K.E. (eds) *Normalisation, Social Integration and Community Services*, Austin, Texas: Pro-Ed. 51–70.

Barclay, P.M. (1982) *Social Workers: Their Role and Tasks (The Barclay Report)*, London: Bedford Square Press.

Barnes, C. (1991) *Disabled People in Britain and Discrimination: A Case for Anti-discrimination Legislation*, London: C Hurst and Co.

Barnes, M. and Bowl, R. (2001) *Taking Over the Asylum.* Basingstoke: Palgrave.

Barry, M. and Hallett, C. (1998) *Social Exclusion and Social Work; Issues of Theory, Policy and Practice,* Lyme Regis: Russell House Publishing.

Bean, P. (1980) *Compulsory Admissions to Mental Hospitals,* Chichester: John Wiley and Sons.

Beaumont, B. (1995) 'Managerialism and the Probation Service', in Williams, B. (ed.) *Probation Values,* Birmingham: Venture. 47–74.

Becker, S., Aldridge, A. and Rearden, C. (1998) *Young Carers and their Families,* London: Blackwell Science.

Beckett, C. (2001) 'The Great Care Proceedings Explosion', *British Journal of Social Work,* 31(2): 493–501.

Begum, N. (1992) 'Disabled Women and the Feminist Agenda', *Feminist Review,* 40: 70–84.

Benn, S.I. (1973) *Social Principles and the Democratic State,* London: Allen & Unwin.

Beresford, B. and Harding, T. (eds) (1993) *A Challenge to Change; Practical Experiences of Building User-Led Services,* London: National Institute for Social Work.

Beresford, P. and Croft, S. (1993) *Citizen Involvement,* Basingstoke: Macmillan.

Beresford, P. and Turner, M. (1997) *Its Our Welfare: Report of the Citizen's Commission on the Future of the Welfare State,* London: National Institute for Social Work.

Bewley, C. (1999) How Do We Support People to Achieve Self-Determination? *VIA Newsletter,* 96.

Bewley, C. (2000) Care Managers Can be Champions for Direct Payments, *Care Plan,* 6:4, 13–6.

Blakemore, K. and Boneham, K. (1994) *Age, Race and Ethnicity: A Comparative Approach,* Buckingham: Open University Press.

Blumental, S.J. (ed.) (1990) *Suicide Over the Life Cycle: Risk Factors, Assessment and Treatment of Suicidal Patients,* Washington, DC: American Psychiatric Press.

Brook, E. and Davis, A. (1985) *Women, the Family and Social Work,* London: Tavistock.

Brown, H. and Walmsley, J. (1997) When 'Ordinary' Isn't Enough: A Review of the Concept of Normalisation, in Bornat, J., Johnson, J., Pereira, C., Pilgrim, D. and Williams, F. (eds) *Community Care: A Reader.* 2nd edn, Basingstoke: Macmillan. 227–36.

Brown, F. (1999) 'Why Person Centred Approaches Build Brighter Futures' *Soundtrack* (National Development Team), 17 (October).

Bryan, B., Dadzie, S. and Scafe, S. (1985) *The Heart of the Race; Black Women's Lives in Britain,* London: Virago.

Buckley, G. (1996) Multiprofessional Learning and Working in the Health Services, in *Opportunities and Obstacles: Perspectives on Interprofessional Education and Training,* Edinburgh: Central Council for Education and Training in Social Work.

Cameron, E., Badger, F. and Evers, H. (1996) 'Ethnicity and Care Management', in Phillips, J. and Penhale, B. (eds) *Reviewing Care Management for Older People,* London, Jessica Kingsley.

Challis, D. and Davies, B. (1986) *Case Management in Community Care*, Aldershot: Gower.

Challis, S., Darton, R., Johnson, L. and Traske, K. (1990) *The Darlington Community Care Project: Supporting Elderly People at Home*, Canterbury, Personal Social Services Research Unit: University of Kent.

Chan, R. and Yu, S. (2000) Chinese Older People in Britain: Double Attachment to Double Detachment, in Warnes, A., Warren, L. and Nolan, M. (eds) *Care Services for Later Life*, London: Jessica Kingsley.

Chelimsky, E. (1981) 'Serving Victims: Agency Incentives and Individual Needs', in Salasin, S.E. (ed.) *Evaluating Victim Services*, Beverly Hills: Sage.

Clarke, L. (1999) *Challenging Ideas in Psychiatric Nursing*, London: Routledge.

Clarke, S. (2000) *Social Work as Community Development; A Management Model for Social Change*, Aldershot: Ashgate.

Connor, A. (1999) 'Community-Based Mental Health Services', in Ulas, M. and Connor, A. (ed.) (1999) *Mental Health and Social Work*, Research highlights in Social Work 28, London: Jessica Kingsley.

Consedine, J. (1995) *Restorative Justice: Healing the Effects of Crime*, Lyttleton, New Zealand: Ploughshares.

Corbett, J. (1995) 'A Proud Label: Exploring the Relationships between Disability, Politics and Gay Pride', *Disability and Society*, 9:3, 343–58.

Coulshed, V. and Orme, J. (1998) *Social Work Practice: An Introduction*. 3rd edn, Basingstoke: Macmillan.

Council of Disabled People (2000) *Double Invisibility*, Coventry: CDP.

Craig, G. and Mayo, M. (1995) *Community Empowerment; A Reader in Participation and Development*, London: Zed Books.

Crow, L. (1996) 'Including All of Our Lives: Renewing the Social Model of Disability', in Barnes, C. and Mercer, G. (eds) *Exploring the Divide; Illness and Disability*, Leeds: The Disability Press.

Dalgleish, L. (2000) *Assessing the Situation and Deciding to Do Something: Risk, Needs and Consequences*, Durban: ISPCAN.

Dalrymple, J. and Burke, B. (1995) *Anti-Oppressive Social Work; Social Care and the Law*, Buckingham: Open University Press.

Davis, A., Ellis, K. and Rummery, K. (1998) *Access to Assessment: Perspectives of Practitioners, Disabled People and Carers*, Bristol: The Policy Press.

Davis, G. (1992) *Making Amends: Mediation and Reparation in Criminal Justice*, London: Routledge.

Decalmer, P. and Glendinning, F. (eds) (1993) *The Mistreatment of Elderly People*, London: Sage.

Department for Education and Skills (2003) *Every Child Matters*, London: The Stationery Office.

Department for Work and Pensions (2002) *Measuring Child Poverty: A Consultation Document*, available at *www.dwp.gov.uk* (accessed 15.11.04).

Department of Health (1991) *Care Management and Assessment: Practitioners' Guide*, London: HMSO.

Department of Health (1994) *Implementing Caring for People: Care Management*, London: DH.

Department of Health (1995) *Child Protection: Messages from Research*, London: HMSO.

Department of Health (1998) *Quality Protects: Framework for Action and Objectives for Social Services for Children*, London: DH.

Department of Health (1999) *Working Together to Safeguard Children*, London: The Stationery Office.

Department of Health (2000) *Framework for the Assessment of Children in Need and their Families*, London: The Stationery Office.

Department of Health (2000) *No Secrets: Guidance on Developing and Implementing Multi-agency Policies and Procedures to Protect Vulnerable Adults from Abuse*, London: The Stationery Office.

Department of Health (2001) *The Children Act Now Messages from Research*, London: The Stationery Office.

Department of Health (2001) *The Service Users Advisory Group Report to the Department of Health 'Nothing About Us Without Us'*, London: DH.

Department of Health (2002) *Direct Payments*, DoH statistical information available online via *www.doh.gov.uk/directpayments* (accessed 26/11/03).

Department of Health (2002) *Requirements for Social Work Training*, London: The Stationery Office.

Department of Health (2003) *The Victoria Climbié Inquiry, Report of an Inquiry by Lord Laming* (Cm. 5730), London: The Stationery Office.

Devore, W. (2001) 'Ethnic Sensitivity: A Theoretical Framework for Social Work Practice', in Dominelli, L., Lorenz, W. and Soydan, H. (eds) *Beyond Racial Divides; Ethnicities in Social Work Practice*, Aldershot: Ashgate. 23–41.

DHSS(1978) Social Service Teams: The Practitioners View, London: HMSO.

Direct Payments Scotland (2002) *DP News: Accessible News about Direct Payments in Scotland*, Edinburgh: Direct Payments Scotland.

Disability Rights Commission (2000) *DRC Disability Briefing: May 2000* (ONLINE: Visited September 2000. URL:

Doel, M. and Shardlow, S.M. (1998) *The New Social Work Practice; Exercises and Activities for Training and Developing Social Workers*, Aldershot: Arena.

Dominelli, L. (1988) *Anti-Racist Social Work*, Basingstoke: Macmillan.

Dominelli, L. (1990) *Women and Community Action*, Birmingham: Venture Press.

Dominelli, L. and McLeod, E. (1989) *Feminist Social Work*, Basingstoke: Macmillan.

Dominey, J. (2002) 'Pre-Sentence reports', in Williams, B. (ed.) *Reparation and Victim-focused Social Work*, London: Jessica Kingsley.

Drake, R.F. (1998) 'Professionals and the Voluntary Sector', in Symonds, A. and Kelly, A. (eds), *The Social Construction of Community Care*, Basingstoke: Macmillan.

Elias, R. (1993) *Victims Still: The Political Manipulation of Crime Victims*, London: Sage.

Emerson, E. (1992) 'What is Normalisation?' in Brown, H. and Smith, H. (eds) *Normalisation: A Reader for the Nineties*, London: Routledge.

Ferguson, H. (1997) 'Protecting Children in New Times: Child Protection and the Risk Society', *Child and Family Social Work*, 2:4, 221–34.

Ferguson, H. (2001) 'Promoting Child Protection, Welfare and Healing: The Case for Developing Best Practice', *Child and Family Social Work*, 6:1, 1–12.

Ferguson, H. (2002) 'Blame Culture in Child Protection', *Guardian Society*, 16 January: 7.

Ferguson, I. (2003) Mental Health and Social Work, in Baillie, D. et al. (eds) (2003) *Social Work and the Law in Scotland*. Open University Publication, Basingstoke: Palgrave.

Fiedler, B. and Twitchin, D. (1992) 'Achieving User Participation' *Living Options in Practice, Project Paper No. 3*. London: King's Fund.

Fisher, M., Newton, C. and Sainsbury, E. (1984) *Mental Health Social Work Observed*, National Institute Social Services Library No. 45, London: George Allen and Unwin.

Fletcher, P. (1998) Focus on Prevention: Back on the Political Agenda, *Working with Older People*, 2:3, 8–12.

Flynn, M. and Flynn, P. (1998) *Think About Having a Learning Disability*, London: Belitha Press.

Foundation for People with Learning Disabilities (2000) *Everyday Choices, Everyday Lives*, London: The Mental Health Foundation.

Franklin, B. (1999) Hard Pressed, National Newspaper Reporting of Social Work and Social Services: *Community Care*.

Frazer, R. and Glick, G. (2000) *Out of Services: A Survey of Social Service Provision for Elderly and Disabled People in Britain*, London: RADAR.

Freire, P. (1972) *Pedagogy of the Oppressed*, Hammondsworth: Penguin.

French, S. (1992) 'Disability, Impairment and or Something in Between?' in Swain, J., Finkelstein, V., French, S. and Oliver, M. (eds), *Disabling Barriers – Enabling Environments*, London: Sage.

French, S. (1994) 'Disabled People and Professional Practice', in *On Equal Terms: Working with Disabled People*, Oxford: Butterworth-Heinemann.

Galaway, B. (1985) 'Victim Participation in the Penal-corrective Process', *Victimology*, 10:1–4, 617–30.

Genders, E. and Player, E. (1995) *Grendon: A Study of a Therapeutic Prison*, Oxford: Clarendon.

Gibbs, J., Evans, M. and Rodway, S. (1987) *Report into the Inquiry into Nye Bevan Lodge*, London: London Borough of Southwark Social Services Department.

Gilroy, P. (1987) *There Ain't No Black in the Union Jack*, London: Century Hutchinson.

Glendinning, C. and Millar, J. (eds) (1987) *Women and Poverty in Great Britain*, Brighton: Wheatsheaf.

Goffman, E. (1961) *Asylums: Essays on the Social Situation of Mental Patients and Other Inmates*, New York: Double Day.

Goldberg, E. and Warburton, W. (1978) *Ends and Means in Social Work*, London: Allen and Unwin.

Goldberg, E., Mortimer, A. and Williams, B. (1970) Helping the Aged: A Field Experiment in Social Work, London: Allen and Unwin.

Goldsmith, M. (1996) *Hearing the Voice of People with Dementia: Opportunities and Obstacles,* London: Jessica Kingsley.

Griffiths, R. (1987) *Agenda for Action,* London: HMSO.

Hallet, C. (ed.) *Women and Social Services,* Hemel Hempstead: Harvester Wheatsheaf.

Hamai, K., Ville, R., Harris, R., Hough, M. and Zvekic, U. (1995) *Probation Around the World,* London: Routledge.

Hanmer, J. and Statham, D. (1988) *Women and Social Work: Towards a Woman Centred Practice,* Basingstoke: Macmillan.

Harris, R. (1995) 'Child Protection, Care and Welfare', in Wilson, K. and James, A. (eds) *The Child Protection Handbook,* London: Balliere Tindall, 27–42.

Hearn, B. (1995) *Child and Family Support and Protection Practical Approach,* London: NCB.

Henderson, R. and Pochin, M. (2001) *A Right Result? Advocacy, Justice and Empowerment,* Bristol: The Policy Press.

Hillman, J. and Mackenzie, M. (1993) *Understanding Field Social Work,* Birmingham: Venture Press.

Hills, J. (1995) *Joseph Rowntree Foundation Inquiry into Income and Wealth (vol. 2),* York: Joseph Rowntree Foundation.

HM Inspectorate of Probation (2003) *Valuing the Victim, Thematic Inspection Report,* London: Home Office.

Hollows, A. (2001) 'The Challenge to Social Work', *Child Psychology and Psychiatry,* 6:1, 1–15.

Hollows, A. (2002) 'Family Support, A Literature Review', *Child and Family Social Work.*

Holman, A. and Bewley, C. (1999) *Funding Freedom 2000: People with Learning Difficulties Getting Direct Payments,* London: VIA.

Holman, B. (2000) *Guardian Newspaper Society,* 4 October.

Holmshaw, J. and Hillier, S. (2000) 'Gender and Culture: A Sociological Perspective to Mental Health Problems in Women', in Kohen, D. (2000) *Women and Mental Health,* London: Routledge, 39–64.

Holton, C. and Raynor, P. (1988) 'Origins of Victims Support Philosophy and Practice', in Maguire, M. and Pointing, J. (eds) *Victims of Crime: A New Deal?* Milton Keynes: Open University Press.

Home Office (1984) *Probation Service in England and Wales: Statement of National Objectives and Priorities,* London: HMSO.

Home Office (1990) *Victim's Charter,* London: Home Office Public Relations Branch.

Home Office (1992) *National Standards for the Supervision of Offenders in the Community,* London: Home Office Probation Service Division.

Home Office (1994) *Three Year Plan for the Probation Service 1995–1998,* London: Home Office.

Home Office (1995) *National Standards for the Supervision of Offenders in the Community,* London: Home Office Probation Service Division.

Home Office (1995a) *Strengthening Punishment in the Community: a Consultation Document* (Cm. 2780), London: HMSO.

Home Office (1995b) *Review of Probation Officer Recruitment and Qualifying Training: Discussion Paper*, London: Home Office Probation Training Unit.

Home Office (2003) *A New Deal for Victims and Witnesses*, London: Home Office.

Home Office (2003a) *Restorative Justice: The Government's Strategy*, London: Home Office Communications Directorate.

Home Office in conjunction with the Department of Health (1992) *Memorandum of Good Practice on Video Recording Interviews With Child Witnesses for Criminal Proceedings*, London: HMSO.

Howe, G. (1998) *Getting into the System: Living with Serious Mental Illness*, London: Jessica Kingsley.

Howlett, M. (1997) Community Care Homicide Inquiries and Risk Assessment, in Kemshall, H. and Pritchard, J. (1997*) Good Practice in Risk Assessment 2 – Protection, Rights and Responsibilities*, London: Jessica Kingsley.

Humphrey, C., Pease, K. and Carter, P. (1993) *Changing Notions of Accountability in the Probation Service*, London: Institute of Chartered Accountants.

Hunt. L., Marshall, M. and Rowlings, C. (eds) (1997) *Past Trauma in Late Life: European Perspectives on Therapeutic Work with Older People*, London: Jessica Kingsley.

Huxley, P. (1985) *Social Work Practice in Mental Health*, Aldershot: Gower Publishing.

Igwe, A. (1998) *Black Survivors 'Hear my Cry', African-Caribbeans and the Impact of Mental Health*, Southampton: The James Wiltshire Trust.

Isaccs, B. and Neville, Y. (1976) *The Measurement of Need in Old People*, Scottish Health Services Studies No. 34, Edinburgh: Scottish Home and Health Department.

Jack, G. (2000) 'Ecological Influences on Parenting and Child Development'. *British Journal of Social Work*, 3:6, 703–20.

Jeewa, S. (1998) *Ethnicity, Disability and Scope: The Case for Embracing Disability Issues*, London: Scope.

Jerrom, C. (2001) Is a £2m Campaign Enough to Revitalise the Social Care Workforce? *Community Care*, 18 October. 1395, 14.

Jones, C. (2001) 'Voices From the Front Line: State Social Workers and New Labour', *British Journal of Social Work*. 31:4.

Jones, K., Brown, J. and Bradshaw, J. (1983) *Issues in Social Policy*, London: Routledge & Kegan Paul.

Katona, C.L.E. (1994) *Depression in Old Age*, Chichester: John Wiley.

Kestenbaum, A. (1992) *Cash for Care: A Report on the Experience of Independent Living Fund Clients*, Nottingham: I.L.F.

Kestenbaum, A. (1999) *What Price Independence? Independent Living and People with High Support Needs*, Bristol: The Policy Press.

Kittwood, T. (1997) *Dementia Reconsidered:The Person Comes First*, Buckingham: Open University Press.

Knight, J. and Brent, M. (1998) *Access Denied: Disabled People's Experience of Social Exclusion*, London: Leonard Cheshire.

Kosh, M. and Williams, B. (1995) *The Probation Service and Victims of Crime: A Pilot Study*, Keele: Keele University Press.

Kuhn, T.S. (1970) *The Structure of Scientific Revolutions*. 2nd edn, Chicago: University of Chicago Press.

Lamb, B. and Layzell, S. (1994) *Disabled in Britain: Vol 1: A World Apart*, London: Scope.

Langan, J. (2000) 'Assessing Risk in Mental Health', in Parsloe, P. (ed.) (2000) *Risk Assessment in Social Care and Social Work*, London: Jessica Kingsley. 153–78.

Langan, M. and Lee, P. (eds) (1989) *Radical Social Work Today*, London: Unwin Hyman.

Launay, G. and Murray, P. (1989) 'Victim/Offender Groups' in Wright, M. and Galaway, B. (eds) *Mediation and Criminal Justice: Victims, Offenders and Community*, London: Sage.

Ledwith, M. (1997) *Participating in Transformation; Towards a Working Model of Community Empowerment*, Birmingham: Venture Press.

Leff, J. (ed.) (1997) *Care in the Community: Illusion or Reality?*, Chichester: John Wiley.

Le Grand, J. and Bartlett, W. (1993) *Quasi Markets and Social Policy*, London: Macmillan.

Levin, E., Sinclair, I. and Gorbach, P. (1988) *Families, Services and Confusion in Old Age*, Aldershot: Gower.

Lewis, J. and Glennerster, H. (1988) *Implementing the New Community Care*, Buckingham: Open University Press.

Liffman, M. (1978) *Power for the Poor; The Family Centre Project, an Experiment in Self-help*, London: Allen and Unwin.

Lipscombe, S. (1997) Homelessness and Mental Health: Risk Assessment, in Kemshall, H. and Pritchard, J. (1997) *Good Practice in Risk Assessment 2 – Protection, Rights and Responsibilities*, London: Jessica Kingsley.

Lishman, J. (ed.) (1993) *A Handbook of Theory for Practice Teachers in Social Work*. London: Jessica Kingsley.

Lister, R. (1997) *Citizenship: Feminist Perspectives*, Basingstoke: Macmillan.

Lloyd, C. (1986) *Response to S. N. O. P.*, Cambridge: Institute of Criminology.

Local Government Association with NHS Confederation and ADSS (2002) *Serving Children Well A New Vision for Children's Services*, London: LGA Publications.

Mackenzie, M. (1975) *Shoulder to Shoulder*, Hammondsworth: Penguin.

MacLeod, J. and Nelson, G. (2000) 'Programs for the Promotion of Family Wellness and the Prevention of Child Maltreatment: A Meta-analytic View', *Child Abuse and Neglect*, 24:9, 1127–49.

Mawby, R.I. and Gill, M.L. (1987) *Crime Victims: Needs, Services and the Voluntary Sector*, London: Tavistock.

Mawby, R.I. and Walklate, S. (1994) *Critical Victimology*, London: Sage.

McCafferty, P. (1994) *Living Independently: A Study of the Housing Needs of Elderly and Disabled People,* London: HMSO.

McCarthy, M. (1999) *Sexuality and Women with Learning Disabilities.* London: Jessica Kingsley.

McCollam, A. (1999) Policy into Practice: Creative Tension or Deadlock? in Ulas, M. and Connor, A. (ed.) (1999) *Mental Health and Social Work,* Research highlights in Social Work 28, London: Jessica Kingsley.

McDonald, A. (1999) *Understanding Community Care: A Guide for Social Workers,* Basingstoke: Macmillan.

McLeod, E. and Bywaters, P. (2000) *Social Work, Health and Equality,* London: Routledge.

Mental Welfare Commission for Scotland (1998*) Annual Report 1997–98,* Edinburgh: Mental Welfare Commission for Scotland.

Miller, J. (1997) *Never Too Young: How Young Children Can Take Responsibility and Make Decisions, a Handbook for Early Years Workers,* London: The National Early Years Network/Save the Children.

Mitchell, G. (ed.) (1968), *The Hard Way Up: The Autobiography of Hannah Mitchell, Suffragette and Rebel,* London: Faber & Faber.

Mitchell, S. (2000) 'Managing Social Services: The Management Challenge of the 1998 Social Services White Paper'. In Hill, M. (ed.) *Local Authority Social Services An Introduction,* Oxford: Blackwell. 179–201.

Morris, J. (1992) 'Personal and Political: A Feminist Perspective on Researching Physical Disability', *Disability, Handicap and Society,* 7:2, 157–66.

Morris, J. (1993) *Independent Lives: Community Care and Disabled People,* Basingstoke: Macmillan.

Morris, J. (1996) *Pride Against Prejudice; Transforming Attitudes to Disability,* London: The Women's Press.

Mullender, A. and Ward, D. (1995) *Self-Directed Groupwork; Users take Action for Empowerment,* London: Whiting and Birch.

Myerhoff, B. (1979) *Number our Days,* New York: Dutton.

Naples, N.A. (1998) *Grassroots Warriors; Activist Mothering, Community Work, and the War on Poverty,* London: Routledge.

Nation, D. (1993) 'A Victim/Offender Group', *Victim Support,* February: 13.

Nirje, B. (1969) 'The Normalisation Principle and its Human Management Implications' in Kugel, R.B. and Wolfensberger, W. (eds) (1969) *Changing Patterns in Residential Services for the Mentally Retarded,* Washington DC: Residential Committee on Mental Retardation.

Nolan, M. (2000) Towards Person-centred Care for Older People, in Warnes, A. Warren, L. and Nolan, M. (eds) (2000) *Care Services for Later Life,* London: Jessica Kingsley.

O'Brien, J. (1987) 'A Guide to Lifestyle Planning: Using the Activities Catalogue to Integrate Services and Natural Support Systems', in Wilcox, B.W. and Bellamy, G.T. (eds) *The Activities Catalogue: An Alternative Curriculum for Youth and Adults With Severe Disabilities,* Baltimore: Brookes.

O'Brien, J. and Lovett, H. (1992) *Finding a Way towards Ordinary Lives: The Contribution of Person Centred Planning.* Harrisburg: Pennsylvania Office of Mental Retardation.

Office of Population Censuses and Surveys (1991) *National Populations Projections 1989 Based,* London: HMSO.

Oliver, M. (1990) *The Politics of Disablement,* Basingstoke: Macmillan.

Oliver, M. and Sapey, B. (1999) *Social Work with Disabled People, 2nd edn,* Basingstoke: Macmillan.

Øvretveit, J. (1993) *Coordinating Community Care; Multi-disciplinary Teams and Care Management,* Buckingham: Open University Press.

Pahl, J. (1989) *Money and Marriage,* Basingstoke: Macmillan.

Parton, N. (2002) 'Protecting Children: A Socio-historical Analysis' in Wilson, K. and James, A. (eds) *The Child Protection Handbook* 2nd edn, London: Balliere Tindall.

Payne, M. (1991) *Modern Social Work Theory: A Critical Introduction,* Basingstoke: Macmillan.

Payne, M. and Shardlow, S.M. (2002) Social Work in the British Isles: Continuities and Differentiations, in Payne, M. and Shardlow, S.M. (eds) *Social Work in the British Isles* 211–46. London: Jessica Kingsley.

Peelo, M., Stewart, J., Stewart, G. and Prior, A. (1992) *A Sense of Justice: Offenders as Victims of Crime,* Wakefield: Association of Chief Officers of Probation.

Petch, A., Cheetham, J., Fuller, R., MacDonald, C. and Myers, F. (1996) *Delivering Community Care,* Edinburgh: The Stationery Office.

Phillips, J. and Penhale, B. (eds) (1996) *Reviewing Care Management for Older People,* London: Jessica Kingsley.

Phillipson, C., Bernard, M., Phillips, J. and Ogg, J. (2001) *The Family and Community Life of Older People: Social Support and Social Networks in Three Urban Areas,* London: Routledge.

Philp, I., Ashe, A. and Lothian, K. (2000) Designing and Implementing a National Service Framework, in Warnes, A., Warren, L. and Nolan, M. (eds) (2000) *Care Services for Later Life,* London: Jessica Kingsley.

Pilgrim, D. and Rogers, A. (1993) *The Sociology of Mental Health and Illness,* Buckingham: Open University Press.

Porter, G. (1990) 'The Consequences of their Behaviour', *Victim Support,* March: 4–5.

Quality Assurance Agency for Higher Education (2000) *Subject Benchmark Statement: Social Policy Administration and Social Work,* Quality Assurance Agency for Higher Education: Gloucester.

Raftery, J. (1996) The Decline of Asylum or the Poverty of the Concept?, in Tomlinson, J. and Carrier, J. (eds) (1996) *Asylum in the Community,* London: Routledge.

Reiner, R. (1992) *The Politics of the Police,* London: Harvester Wheatsheaf.

Revans, L. (2000) 'Commission Seeks to Add to its Remit', *Community Care,* 14–20 September, 12.

Richards, S. (2000) Bridging the Divide: Elders and the Assessment Process, *British Journal of Social Work,* 30: 37–49.

Richmond, M. (1917) *Social Diagnosis*, New York: Russell Sage Foundation.

Riddell, S., Stalker, K., Wilkinson, H. and Baron, S. (1997) *The Meaning of the Learning Society for Adults with Learning Difficulties*. Glasgow: University of Glasgow.

Rimmer, A. and Harwood, K. (2004) *Citizen Participation in the Education and Training of Social Workers*, Social Work Education.

Rogers, A. (1990) 'Policing Mental Disorder: Controversies, Myths and Realities', *Social Policy and Administration*, 24:3, 226–37.

Rogers, A. and Pilgrim, D. (1996) *Mental Health Policy in Britain, A Critical Introduction*, Basingstoke: Macmillan.

Rose, W. (2000) 'Assessing Children in Need and their Families: An Overview of the Framework', in Horwath, J. (ed.) The *Child's World: Assessing Children in Need, The Reader*. London: NSPCC. 29–60.

Rowlings, C. (1985) 'Practice in Field Care', in Lishman, J. (ed.) *Research Highlights in Social Work 3: Developing Services for the Elderly*, London: Kogan Page.

Rowlings, C. (1995) 'Elder Abuse in Context', in Clough, R. (ed.) *Elder Abuse and the Law*, London: Action on Elder Abuse.

Royal Commission on Law Relation to Mental Illness and Mental Deficiency (1957) *Report*, London: HMSO.

Russell, J. (1990) *Home Office Funding of Victim Support Schemes: Money Well Spent?*, Research and Planning Unit Paper 58. London: Home Office.

Ryan T. (1997) Risk, Residential Services and People with Mental Health Needs, in Kemshall, H. and Pritchard, J. (ed.) (1994) *Good Practice in Risk Assessment and Risk Management 2*. London: Jessica Kingsley, 159–73.

Sackett, D.L., Roseberg, W.M., Gray, J.A.M., Haynes, R.B. and Richardson, W.S. (1996) 'Evidence Based Medicine: What it is and What it isn't – its About Integrating Individual Clinical Expertise and the Best External Evidence', *British Medical Journal*, 7023, 71–2.

Sampson, A. (1994) *Acts of Abuse: Sex Offenders and the Criminal Justice System*, London: Routledge.

Sampson, A. and Smith, D. (1992) 'Probation and Community Crime Prevention', *Howard Journal of Criminal Justice*, 31:2, 105–19.

Sanders, A. and Senior, P. (1994) *Jarvis Probation Officers' Manual*, 5th edn, Sheffield: PAVIC.

Sanderson, H., Kennedy, J., Ritchie, P. and Goodwin, G. (1997) *People, Plans and Possibilities: Exploring Person-centred Planning*, Edinburgh: SHS.

Sayce, L. (2000) *From Psychiatric Patient to Citizen, Overcoming Discrimination and Social Exclusion*, Basingstoke: Macmillan.

Scottish Executive (2000) *Report from the Joint Future Group*, Edinburgh: Scottish Executive.

Scottish Executive (2000) *The Same as You? A Review of Services for People with Learning Disabilities*. Edinburgh: The Stationery Office.

Scottish Executive (2004a) *Adults with Learning Disabilities Implementation of 'The Same as You?' Scotland 2003.*
http://www.scotland.gov.uk/stats/bulletins/00326–00.asp

Scottish Executive (2004b) *Direct Payments Policy and Practice Guidance Update.* Circular No. CCD 1/2004. Edinburgh: Scottish Executive Health Department.

Scottish Office (1996) *Guidance on the Care Programme Approach for People with Severe and Enduring Mental Illness Including Dementia,* Edinburgh: The Scottish Office.

Secretaries of State for Health, Social Security, Wales and Scotland (1989) *Caring for People: Community Care in the Next Decade and Beyond,* London: HMSO.

Secretary of State for Social Services (1988) *Report into the Inquiry of Child Abuse in Cleveland* (Cm. 412), London: HMSO.

Seebohm, F. (1968) Report of the Committee on Local Authority and Allied Personal Social Services (Seebohm Report) (Cm. 3703), London: HMSO.

Shapland, J. (1988) 'Fiefs and Peasants: Accomplishing Change for Victims in the Criminal Justice System', in Maguire, M. and Pointing, J. (eds) *Victims of Crime: a New Deal?* Milton Keynes: Open University Press. 187–94.

Sheldon, B. and Chilvers, R. (2000) *Evidence-Based Social Care.* Lyme Regis: Russell House Publishing.

Sheppard, M. (1991) *Mental Health Work in the Community: Theory and Practice in Social Work and Community Psychiatric Nursing,* Basingstoke: Macmillan.

Sheppard, M. (1999) Maternal Depression in Child and Family Care, in Ulas, M. and Connor, A. (ed.) (1999) *Mental Health and Social Work,* London: Jessica Kingsley.

Silburn, L., Dookun, D. and Jones, C. (1994) 'Innovative Practice', in French, S. (ed.) *Equal Terms: Working with Disabled People,* Oxford: Heinemann.

Sim, A.J., Milner, J., Love, J. and Lishman, J. (1998) 'Definitions of Need: Can Disabled People and Care Professionals Agree?' *Disability and Society,* 13:1, 53–74.

Simons, K. (1993) *Citizen Advocacy: The Inside View,* Bristol: Norah Fry Research Centre.

Sinclair, I., Parker, P., Leat, D. and Williams, J. *The Kaleidoscope of Care: A Review of Research of Welfare Provision for Elderly People,* London: HMSO.

Smith, H. and Brown, H. (1992) 'Defending Community Care: Can Normalization do the Job?' *British Journal of Social Work,* 22:6, 685–93.

Smull, M. and Harrison, S.B. (1992) *Supporting People with Severe Reputations in the Community.* Alexandria, VA: NASMRPD.

Snell, J. (2000) 'The Right to Freedom', *The Guardian,* November 1, 6.

Social Services Inspectorate (2000) *New Directions for Independent Living: Inspection of Independent Living Arrangements for Younger Disabled People,* London: DH.

Social Services Inspectorate (1997) *The Cornerstones of Care: Inspection of Care Planning for Older People,* London: DH.

Social Services Inspectorate and Social Work Services Group (1991) *Care Management and Assessment: Summary of Practice Guidance,* London: HMSO.

Spratt, T. (2001) 'The Influence of Child Protection Orientation on Child Welfare Protection', *British Journal of Social Work*. 31: 933–54.

Stalker, K. and Reddish, S. (1994) *Supporting Disabled People in Scotland*, A Report to The Scottish Office, Social Work Research Centre, Stirling: University of Stirling.

Stevenson, O. (1999) 'Social Work with Children and Families', in Stevenson, O. *Child Welfare in the United Kingdom 1948–1988*, Oxford: Blackwell.

Stevenson, O. and Parsloe, P. (1993) *Community Care and Empowerment*, York: Joseph Rowntree Foundation.

Stuart, O. (1993) 'Double Oppression: An Appropriate Starting Point?' in Swain, J., Finkelbain, V., French, S. and Oliver, M. (eds), *Disabling Barriers: Enabling Environments*, London: Sage.

Sturges, P.J. (1996) Care Management Practice: Lessons from the USA, in Clark, C. and Lapsley, I. (ed.) (1996) *Planning and Costing Community Care*, London: Jessica Kingsley.

Tanner, D. (2001) Partnership in Prevention: Messages From Older People, in White, V. and Harris, J. (eds) *Developing Good Practice in Community Care*, London: Jessica Kingsley.

Tester, S. and Meredith, B. (1987) Ill-informed? *A Study of Information and Support for Elderly People in the Inner City*, London: Policy Study Institute.

The Scottish Office (1996) *1995 Health in Scotland*, Edinburgh: The Stationery Office.

Thoburn, J. (1996) 'The Community Child Care Team', in Davies, M. (ed.) *The Companion to Social Work*, Oxford: Blackwell, 290–296.

Thoburn, J. (2001) 'The Good News on Children's Services', *Community Care*, 1394, 11–7.

Thomas, C. (1999) *Female Forms: Experiencing and Understanding Disability.* Buckingham: Open University Press.

Thompson, A. (1999) 'Carry on Caring', *Community Care*, 25 November: 28–9.

Thompson, D. (1993) Learning *Disabilities: The Fundamental Facts*, London: Mental Health Foundation.

Thompson, N. (1997) *Anti-Discriminatory Practice*, Basingstoke: Macmillan.

Thompson, N. (1998) Social Work with Adults, in Adams, R., Dominelli, L. and Payne, M. (eds) (1998) *Social Work: Themes, Issues and Critical Debates*, Basingstoke: Macmillan.

Thompson, N. (2000) *Understanding Social Work: Preparing for Practice*, Basingstoke: Macmillan.

Towell, D. (1990) 'Achieving Strategic Change: A Principled Agenda for the 1990s', in Booth, T. (ed.) *Better Lives; Changing Services for People with Learning Difficulties*, Sheffield: Joint Unit for Social Services Research.

Townsley, R. and Macadam, M. (1996) *Choosing Staff: Involving People with Learning Difficulties in Staff Recruitment*, Bristol: The Policy Press.

Trotter, N. (1990) 'Strangeways Visit', *Victim Support*, March, 4.

Tudor, B. (2002) 'Probation Work With Victims of Crime', in Williams, B. (ed.) *Reparation and Victim-focused Social Work*, London: Jessica Kingsley.

Tunstill, J. (1997) 'Implementing the Family Support Clauses of the 1989 Children Act', in Parton, N. (ed.) *Child Protection and Family Support: Tensions, Contradictions and Possibilities.* London: Routledge. 57–84.

Tunstill, J. (2000) 'Child Care'. In Hill, M. (ed.) (2000) *Local Authority Social Services: An Introduction,* Oxford: Blackwell.

Tunstill, J. and Aldgate, J. (2000) *Services for Children in Need: From Policy to Practice,* London: The Stationery Office.

Ulas, M. and Connor, A. (ed.) (1999) *Mental Health and Social Work,* London: Jessica Kingsley.

Utting, W. (1995) *Family and Parenthood: Supporting Families, Preventing Breakdown,* York: Joseph Rowntree Foundation.

Vassilas, A. and Morgan, H.G. (1997) 'Suicide in Avon', *British Journal of Psychiatry,* 453–5.

Victim Support (1995) *The Rights of Victims of Crime,* London: Victim Support.

Walker, C., Ryan, T. and Walker, A. (1995) 'A Step in the Right Direction: People With Learning Difficulties Moving Into the Community', *Health and Social Care in the Community,* 3:4, 249–60.

Walklate, S. (1989) *Victimology: the Victim and the Criminal Justice Process,* London: Unwin Hyman.

Ward, D. (2000) 'Totem not Token: Groupwork as a Vehicle for User Participation', in Kemshall, H. and Littlechild, R. (eds) *User Involvement and Participation in Social Care,* London: Jessica Kingsley. 45–64.

Waterhouse, L. and McGhee, J. (2002) 'Social Work with Children and Families', in Adams, R., Dominelli, L. and Payne, M. (eds) (2000), *Social Work: Themes, Issues and Critical Debates,* 2nd edn, Basingstoke: Palgrave. 273–96.

Watters, C. (1996) Representations and Realities: Black People, Community Care and Mental Illness, in Ahmad, W.I.U. and Atkin, K. (1996) *'Race' and Community Care,* Buckingham: Open University Press.

White, S. (1996) Regulating Mental Health and Motherhood, *Critical Social Policy,* 16:1, 67–95.

Williams, B. (1995) 'Probation Values in Work with Prisoners', in Williams, B. (ed.) (1995) *Probation Values,* Birmingham: Venture.

Williams, B. (1999) *Working with Victims of Crime: Policies, Politics and Practice,* London: Jessica Kingsley.

Williams, B. (2000) Victims of Crime and the New Youth Justice, in Goldson, B. (ed.) (1995) *The New Youth Justice.* Lyme Regis. Russell House Publishing.

Williams, F. (1989) *Social Policy: A Critical Introduction,* Cambridge: Polity Press.

Williams, V. (1999) 'Give Us Paid Work and Stop Labelling Us', *Community Care 'Inside Learning Difficulties' Supplement,* 23 February: 4–5.

Winchester, R. (2000) 'Report Exposes the Same Old Attitudes', *Community Care,* July: 11.

Wolfensberger, W. (1972) *The Principle of Normalisation in Human Services,* Toronto: National Institute in Mental Retardation.

Wolfensberger, W. (1980) 'The Definition of Normalisation: Update, Problems, Disagreements and Misunderstandings', in Flynn, R.J. and Nitsch, K.E. (eds) (1980) *Normalisation, Social Integration and Community Services,* Baltimore: University Park Press.

Woodhouse, D. and Pengelly, P. (1991) *Anxiety and the Dynamics of Collaboration,* Aberdeen: Aberdeen University Press.

Younghusband, E. (1964) *Social Work and Social Change,* London: Allen & Unwin.

Younghusband, E. (1981) The Newest Profession, A Short History of Social Work, London: *Community Care.*

Zarb, G. and Nadash, P. (1994) *Cashing in on Independence: Comparing the Costs and Benefits of Cash and Services,* Derbyshire: BCODP.

Zedner, L. (2002) 'Victims', in Maguire, M., Morgan, R. and Reiner, R. (eds) *The Oxford Handbook of Criminology,* Oxford: Clarendon Press.

Useful websites

For the social worker in the twenty-first century the internet is an invaluable tool. Whether you are a busy practitioner looking for evidence to support and guide practice, a student looking for information for an assignment, or a professional based overseas seeking an insight into the organisation and structure of social work in the UK the internet is an essential resource. It can, however, be a confusing and time consuming resource. The following annotated list aims to guide readers to a number of key sites which provide reliable starting points to effectively using the internet as a social work tool.

Career, education and training resources

www.gscc.org.uk – The website of the General Social Care Council. The council operates as the regulator of social work and the social care workforce in England. Here you can find information on registration of social workers and codes of practice alongside information about education and training. There are links to the regulatory bodies for Northern Ireland, Scotland and Wales.

www.socialworkcareers.co.uk – This website provides information on careers in social work and guidance on studying for the social work qualification.

Official government resources

www.doh.gov.uk – The website of the Department of Health. This large site offers full text documents published by the department alongside a range of guidance and policy related to health and social care.

www.dfes.gov.uk – The website for the Department of Education and Skills. This large site offers full text documents published by the department alongside a range of guidance and policy related to education and social care. For example the government green paper on the future of children's social work, 'Every Child Matters' can be found here.

http://www.publications.parliament.uk – This site provides full texts of bills before parliament.

Gateway sites

These sites are a good starting point when looking for information or researching a specific issue.

www.scie.org.uk – The website of the Social Care Institute for Excellence is not of itself a gateway site but does offer social workers a range of useful resources and links to a wide range of useful sites. The organisation aims to collect and synthesise knowledge about what works in social care.

www.elsc.org.uk – This is the electronic Library for Social Care, which provides access to databases such as caredata, full text publications, and information on research findings and publications.

http://www.be-evidence-based.com – This site aims to make readily available research findings on what works for busy social work practitioners. The site allows practitioners or users to search for a summary of key research findings within social care linked to implications for practice.

www.sosig.ac.uk – This site is the Social Science Information Gateway, which collects and organises selected high quality information on social science.

www.rip.org.uk – Research in Practice is a site which brings together research and policy specifically focusing on meeting the needs of children and families.

www.makingresearchcount.org.uk – a national collaborative research dissemination intitiative, established by a consortium of universities and developed by regional centres.

www.swap.ac.uk – SWAP is the Social Policy and Social Work subject centre with the Higher Education Academy.

Care Leavers Association, c/o Jim Goddard, PO Box 179, Shipley, BD18 3WX. *www.careleavers.com*

CATS Group. *Citizens as Trainers*, c/o Pat Garratt, School of Community, Health & Social Care, University of Salford.

Distress Awareness Training Agency, Andrew Hughs, *sun@artofawareness.co.uk*

Frampton, P. (2001) Care Leavers Association, c/o Jim Goddard, PO Box 179, Shipley, BD18 3WX. *www.careleavers.com*

Social Action Journal. (1995) Centre for Social Action, De-Montford University, dmu.ac.uk/~csa.

SUN. Survivors United Network, c/o Andrew Hughs *sun@artofawareness.co.uk*
The Mental Health Foundation *www.mentalhealth.org.uk*

Specific sites

www.jrf.org.uk – The Joseph Rowntree Foundation is an independent social policy research and development charity supporting projects in housing, social care and social policy. This site forms part of the foundation's aim to ensure the findings of the research programme are fully disseminated.

www.scmh.org.uk – The Sainsbury Centre for Mental Health is a charity, which works to improve the quality of life for people with severe mental health problems. The site has a range of resources including a database, *www.mentalhealthdata.org.*

Electronic journals

www.criticalsocialwork.com – Several print journals offer tables of contents and abstracts free over the Internet but Critical Social Work is an electronic journal, which offers full text of all articles free on the internet.

Discussion Lists

www.jiscmail.ac.uk – This site hosts two discussion lists of particular interest. The first, uksocwork, is for social work academics, practitioners and students in the UK to discuss issues of mutual interest, whilst intsocwork is directed to those with a more international focus.

Exploring further

www.vts.rdn.ac.uk – For those new to accessing and evaluating social work information on the Internet, Angela Upton, of the Social Care Institute for Excellence has developed a free teach yourself tutorial, 'The Internet Social Worker', an excellent resource for making the most of what the internet has to offer.

Index